Bad Beaver Tales

Love and Life in Downeast Maine

Carol Leonard

Bad Beaver Publishing
222 Red Bridge Road
Ellsworth, ME 04605
603.568.1487

Library of Congress Cataloging-in-Publication Data
Leonard, Carol
Bad beaver tales, love and life in downeast maine / Carol Leonard (1950 –)
pages cm

ISBN 978-1-790-70731-7

Second Edition

Cover design by Carol Leonard
Cover photo **"Hillbilly Hot Tub"** by Tom Lajoie
Carol and Tom's wedding photo by Anne Staveley Dickinson, 2005
Photo **"Crow Flies Home"** by Ariella Fay Neville, 2014
All photos property of Bad Beaver Farm unless otherwise stated.

Also by Carol Leonard

The Women's Wheel of Life (co-authored with Elizabeth Davis)

First published by in 1996 by Viking Penguin

Women of the Thirteenth Moon,

A Baby Boomer's Survival Guide to Menopause

"Medea" (short story)

The Beauty Girls

Lady's Hands, Lion's Heart, A Midwife's Saga

DEDICATION

To my sweet husband, Tom Lajoie, who embodies the true spirit of the pioneer man who can fix anything...including a broken heart.

I love you, Bubbalouie.

Life with you continues to be a remarkable adventure.

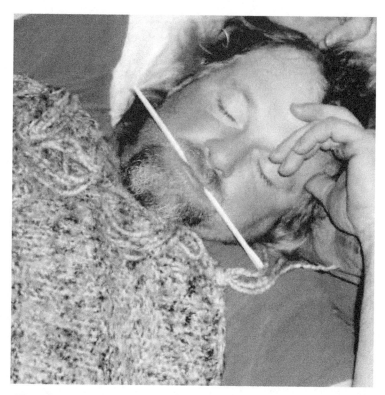

Tom Lajoie ~ Woodsman Extraordinaire in a rare repose.

CONTENTS

Winter

Spring Reprise

PROLOGUE

I became a widow at thirty-seven years of age and my world came crashing down. This is what I wrote in the Epilogue of my memoir of that time, **Lady's Hands, Lion's Heart, A Midwife's Saga**:

"I lost my mind for quite some time. I knew I had to stop working before I hurt someone. My grief was much too raw for me to be able to take care of others. I had to heal myself. I built a lodge out of woven saplings at the base of the Tree where my husband died. I covered the saplings with tarps and made a fire pit in the center. I stayed there for the better part of a year without speaking much.

Looking back on this, it seems a little insane, but I had the support of my family and friends. It was a painful time but also a time of intense healing, living in the beauty of the forest. The Tree and the deer and the pileated woodpeckers and the coydog all healed me. I began to recover.

I had a spiritual decade, where I delved deeply into women's spirituality and the blood mysteries. I went back into midwifery practice in the late nineties. I opened my birth center, Longmeadow Farm Birthing Home, and attended births at my home.

I'm OK; I made it through. I'm happy now. I am married to a wild French Canadian redneck builder, Tom Lajoie. Tom is eighteen years my junior. Actually, Tom and his family lived across the street from Ken and me when we lived in the little farmhouse in Concord. Little Tommy was my "handy-boy" when he was young; he stacked my wood. He says he's been in love with me since he was eleven.

Tom and I have a four-hundred-acre parcel of land in Ellsworth, Maine, that we are making into a tree farm. We are doing sustainable harvesting, and Tom has a sawmill and a shingle-mill there. We have named the land Bad Beaver Farm."

Tom and I reunited in 1995 when he was 27 years old and I was 45. (I know…I know…I've heard all the cradle-robbing snide remarks, believe me. But he was a grown man by then and I fell tumultuously, head-over-heels in love with him.) A decade later, we had the unbelievable good fortune to purchase 400 acres of wilderness in Downeast Maine. The land has miles of untamed forests and rivers and old pastures and beaver flowages…*lots* of beaver ponds. The land is inhabited by deer and moose, bears and coyotes, herons and owls and wild turkeys—and now us.

What I didn't know when we bought the land was how much it was going to mean to me—how much it was going to form and change me. The primitive wildness of the land has given me permission to recreate myself, yet again.

In my youth, I was a "challenging" child. I had the powerful, expansive experience of coming of age in the 1960s. The 1960s were an intense time of freedom and experimentation and self-discovery for me. In my teens, I became a card-carrying Flower Child. I was at Woodstock, for godsake. Actually, I'm pretty sure I was at Woodstock on the day that Tom was born. It is quite possible that it was on the day he was born that I accidentally ripped off three of my toenails.

I was sliding in the mud on a hill on Max Yeager's farm with a bunch of newfound hippie friends. The mud was so cold, we didn't realize until too late that there was an old dump underneath it—an old trash heap full of jagged cans and glass. I didn't feel a thing until three of my toenails had been sheared off. The drive back home to New Hampshire was miserable. I sat in the backseat of the car, silently weeping in pain with my friend and festival mate, Dickey Ladeau. Dickey was crying too because he had taken bad acid and was being drafted into the Vietnam War the next day. My toes eventually healed and the nails grew back. Dickey came back home a year later in a body bag.

As the 1960s rushed on, I became more daring. When I was seventeen, I hitchhiked from Manchester, New Hampshire to a family planning clinic in Berkeley, California to get an experimental IUD inserted. On my travels back home, I ran into a very naughty girl named Nancy in Boulder, Colorado. She introduced me to the fine art of hopping freight trains. She taught me how to befriend the brakemen to tell us what we needed to know. We hopped trains for months all through the wild West until we got arrested in Green River, Wyoming and were put in jail for two weeks. Badlands for bad girls. That was on Thanksgiving Day, 1967. My mother still talks about it.

But then...I became a Responsible Adult. I got a BS in Natural History. I had a child. I became a midwife. I delivered my first baby when I was twenty-four years old, and went on to deliver over 1000 babies safely in their own homes—at the same time being immersed in the privileged, conservative life of an obstetrician's wife. For over a decade, my life was skiing and sailing and gardening and genteel cocktail parties (well, granted...some of the parties were not all that genteel). I wore pink wrap-around skirts and white silk blouses.

And then my husband, Ken, killed himself. Out in our back woods, at a special place we called The Tree, my gorgeous, funny, brilliant husband took his boot off, put a 12-gauge shotgun in his mouth and pulled the trigger with his toe. A neighbor who was cross-country skiing for the first time in her life skied down our trail and came upon a headless corpse at the base of The Tree. Blood and brains splattered everywhere in the snow. I still give thanks unto the heavens that it wasn't me skiing that day.

I spiraled down into the deepest, blackest anguish imaginable—a bottomless abyss of relentless sorrow. My grief lasted a decade.

But life can be devious. What seems like an unsurvivable tragedy can turn into a miraculous gift. Almost three decades later, I am with Tom, and on our land. I have the opportunity to experience the intense freedom and experimentation that I had in the beginning of my life—only now I am recreating myself, one more time, as my life winds down.

At Bad Beaver, Tom is teaching me how to shoot and hunt. I taught myself how to trap beaver. I learned how to skin and flesh and dry beaver pelts. I know how to prepare beaver meat for our freezer. I can fish for brook trout out of my kayak in the beaver ponds. I can forage for wild mushrooms and medicinal plants that I use to make healing tinctures. I ride the old fat-tire Schwinn that Tom found at the dump, bouncing along the miles of gravel roads that Tom put in on our land, with our dogs trotting deliriously beside me. I can snowshoe and track moose and deer and coyotes and bears (our bears have indigo colored scat in the late summer from all the blueberries they consume).

And the beavers! Those never-ending, undefeatable, smart, adorable, destructive effing rodents. We will never be beaver-less. We just discovered another huge beaver pond upstream from their last known address. This keeps me strong. I am making beautiful beaver fur hats and bedspreads from their luxurious pelts.

So, this book is a chronicle of my growth in my later years, mishaps and successes made along the way, the evolution of my relationship with Tom and our dedication to being humble stewards of our land. The following tales are a collection of stories not just about Bad Beaver the place, but stories that meander around in my life, past and present. At the same time, Bad Beaver is where it all leads.

As a writer friend says, "These stories from Bad Beaver are, at turns, brave, beautiful and just plain badass."

I hope you have as much fun reading my stories as I had writing them.

Carol Leonard
Ellsworth, Maine

SPRING

SPRING

HOW CAROL AND TOM HOOKED UP...FINALLY

**Carol and Tom on their wedding day ~
July 3, 2005, Ellsworth, Maine**

I used to live in a funky little farmhouse in New Hampshire with my late husband, an obstetrician/gynecologist from the Midwest whom I adored. I was in my late 20s and my 30s then. Across the street from our house was a sizable French Canadian family with a passel of rowdy, adolescent boys. The youngest of the Lajoie boys became my "handy boy." Little Tommy did chores around our house when he was eleven. He would mow the lawn

3

and stack the firewood and trim branches, because my husband was away at the hospital a great deal of the time. Tommy was an adorable, sweet boy with very blond hair and bright blue eyes and freckles.

Then, my beloved husband committed suicide. I was beyond bereft, nearly mute with grief. I had a bigger farm, fields and vegetable gardens in Hopkinton. Tom was in his late teens then, and he came back to help me with the upkeep of the farm. He was a hard worker. He plowed the gardens and mowed the fields and felled trees for firewood. He was always courteous and sweet. He used to arrive at the farm on a tri-cycle motorcycle he had built out of an old VW bug with a chopper front.

One day Tom asked me if I would go with him to the Loudon motorcycle races. This surprised me, but I declined, saying I was a grieving widow and didn't think it would be appropriate. Besides, I couldn't really picture myself riding on the back of a homemade chopper with a boy half my age. Not after what I'd been through.

Tom told me he was going away to the Pacific Northwest to work as a whitewater guide. I was sad to see him go, and for some reason I gave him an Egyptian ankh earring I had, to take with him. The ankh represents "forever." I told him to wear it to keep him safe. I didn't see Tom again for almost ten years.

In my mid-40s, I decided to end a long, self-imposed sentence of celibacy (well, long for *me* anyway). As soon as I made that decision, men started coming around like moths to a candle flame (amazing how that happens...must be pheromones). There were three men: one was probably, in retrospect, a charming serial killer; one was a crazy, very screwed-up artist; and one was a wealthy insurance company president who had a summer home on the ocean near mine on Contention Cove in Surry, Maine. I decided to go for the safety of wealth.

The CEO was supposed to pick me up with his yacht at my little cottage in Surry. I was planning to go to his island for the weekend. As I stood on the bank overlooking the cove, there was a tremendous storm brewing. The sky darkened and opened up with a frightful gale. I realized the sea was way too rough for him to make it to my shore.

I thought, "This is odd, I wonder what this is all about." I turned to go back inside.

At this moment, a beat-up black pick-up truck pulled into my driveway. A gorgeous blond, bearded man stepped out. I stood frozen in my tracks.

"Tommy?" He grinned that beautiful smile that I would recognize anywhere. Tears sprang to my eyes, how wonderful to see him again! As we hugged, I noticed he was wearing the ankh.

We picked mussels from the shore and cooked them in garlic and wine and sat in the wind on the beach eating them. Tom looked at me with those ridiculously soulful blue eyes.

He said, "I've been in love with you since I was eleven. Is it safe to love you now?"

My own eyes widened in realization of what was about to happen.

I said, "Good timing, Mr. Lajoie."

Early Carol and Tommy (he is still wearing the ankh earring here)

The CEO called the cottage the next morning and said the storm was over and that he would come get me. I told him I had "company."

He paused. Then, with an angry edge in his voice, he said, "Well, that was *fast*."

I said, "Yep. Dark Horse at the eleventh hour…won by a nose."

WHEN TOM FRIED BACON NAKED

Several days later, when we came up for air, I smelled coffee brewing and bacon frying, so I jumped out of bed and ran down the stairs. I grinned to see Tom standing buck-naked in front of the funky old white porcelain electric cook stove that came with the camp. He was frying bacon. He has such a great ass. It is high and round and solid. I couldn't resist. I leaned over to kiss his butt. When I did this, his penis made contact with the metal strip that rimmed the top of the stove.

What we didn't know at the time was that the stove had a serious electrical short. A vicious electric shock shot through his unprotected phallus. He roared and reared back. That fabulous, muscular ass made solid contact with my nose.

I heard a definite "crunch" and started seeing stars. *"OWWWWWW!"*

I wailed pitifully, "Oh god, Tom, I think you may have broken my nose!"

As it turned out, my nose was only bruised; it got a little black and blue. More bruised was our dignity.

That is how I got the fabulous new 6-burner GAS cook stove that is in the cottage today. I highly recommend it—electric penile shock therapy.

Moral of the story: Never cook bacon naked.

NEW HAMPSHAH

When Tom and I first reconnected, he was building spec houses for his friend Milos, a Yugoslavian entrepreneur in Orono. Tom was a bright, energetic young man attending his senior year at the University of Maine in Orono when Milos hired him to build his microbrewery, The Bear Brew Pub.

Tom and I used to sleep upstairs above the pub in the grain room with the delicious smell of the fermenting hops that Milos used to make his micro-brews. Tom was building the bar, and I painted a mural in the pub of Breughel's Peasant Wedding, except I replaced all the people in the painting with the faces of the local inhabitants of Milos's bar. It was a heady time for us and Tom proved to be an, um...very *innovative* lover. It got pretty hot in that grain room. We were so enraptured with each other that it didn't matter to us that we were sleeping nestled in bags of hops, listening to drunk college kids at night "bowling" using beer bottles as candle pins in the alleyway downstairs.

Tom was already getting a reputation in Orono as a self-made man and phenomenal "economy of motion" builder. Beginning at the ripe age of twelve, Tom had sought out knowledgeable teachers who could tutor him in the best skills of the building trades. Within a decade, he had mastered the expertise needed for plumbing, electrical, automotive and welding skills to an insane degree. He spent a year in the Pacific Northwest studying framing from the best—a man he admired and affectionately called "The Captain." Under the Captain's strict tutelage, Tom became one of the fastest and most accurate framers around.

Honestly, after being with him for over twenty years now—I think Tom may be some sort of building/math savant.

It was when I was first with him in Orono that he was befriended by the older tradesmen at the infamous Pat's Pizza. At Pat's Pizza, there was a 6:00 AM Coffee Crew that met every morning as a ritual before going to their respective jobs. It was a group of older, hard-working, local gentlemen who sat four to a booth and downed their coffees and bickered and bitched at each other good-naturedly. One morning as Tom was getting some caffeine to go, the mason, Louie Rosebush, who was sitting with the established old guard, shouted, "Hey, New Hampshah, you sit right heah!" He made all his friends squish together in the booth to make room for Tom to join them.

The Coffee Crew had taken a liking to young Tommy, I imagine because they saw the raging talent roiling just under the surface. These men took to checking up on Tom no matter where he was working. They all called Tom "New Hampshah." Tom would grin, bursting with pride at having been accepted by these self-made men. He would get rather misty-eyed talking about Louie and his gang and how much respect he had for these elder men who had the old knowledge of how to do things, and how he regretted that those ways would be gone when they died. This made my love for him soar and my heart full, because young Tom didn't know it yet—but he was one of those men too.

RIPYOURJEANSOFF GORGE

Some people think that I derailed studious Tom's college career, but that's not true. I didn't. It happened before I was even on the scene. I blame it on the lure of the river. I blame it solely on whitewater fever.

At the time, Tom was a Maine licensed whitewater guide and, as a senior at the University of Maine, he had created a self-designed major he called "Adventure Carpentry," which fulfilled a semester's worth of credits while combining carpentry and outdoor education.

He worked for a rafting company named Unicorn, taking screaming people down the West Branch of the Penobscot River. The West Branch had a Class IV rapid that ripped down a steep gorge that came out of the Ripogenus Dam. All the guides called it the "Rip-your-jeans-off gorge" because the water was so crazy violent.

Ripogenus Gorge is a deep rock-walled canyon that is 700 feet wide and a mile long. It is the most spectacularly rugged river canyon in the Northeast. The sheer granite walls rise several hundred feet directly out of the water. Immediately below Ripyourjeansoff is a Class V rapid called The Cribworks. The name comes from wooden structures filled with rocks known as cribs, built in years-gone-by by loggers to ensure that logs passed through the rapid freely. The Cribworks is the Northeast's most notorious and difficult rapid to navigate.

Maine whitewater guides running the Cribworks had to have a special license to bring people down it. Tom was licensed to run it, so occasionally he had to take a greener guide's raft down the Class V rapid for him. Tom was also an extreme whitewater kayaker, and he and his paddling buds used to run Ripyourjeansoff Gorge and the Cribworks just for fun.

When Tom and I had been together for exactly twelve days, he said he'd like for me to come along on his raft trip down the West Branch. I was delighted, although I had never been on whitewater before. We had been sleeping in his tent outside of the guides' loft in Millinocket because the loft was so grungy with potential creepy-crawlies that it was nauseating. Besides, the stench of smelly, unwashed poly-pro practically gave me a nosebleed.

The first time I looked down on Ripyourjeansoff Gorge from the trail above, I got vertigo. The sheer walls of the canyon from where I was standing plummeted down hundreds of feet to a ribbon of roiling, angry whitewater. There were what appeared to be several dark beetles flying down the rapid called "Exterminator"—the beetles being the minuscule looking rafts full of shrieking people. I couldn't believe we were soon going to be flushing down that chute. I was dizzy with anxiety. Tom was grinning an especially evil grin right then.

"Seriously, is this a sane idea?" I asked.

"Oh, sure. Nobody ever gets killed on this run."

I had the sinking "famous last words" mantra playing in my head.

But flush down the chute we did. I have to admit it was exhilarating. I was grinning and nervously laughing the whole way through Exterminator. Tom was great. He landed the raft precisely where he wanted it on the run and spun into eddies when he could. There were six others in our raft, and when we would come to a particularly gnarly section, Tom would scream at us, ***"Paddle! Paddle! Paddle!"*** And the seven of us would paddle for all we were worth. Then Tom would smile and say we did great.

We got out above the Cribworks to "scout" the run. Tom was explaining to us how to read the water. He was talking about smooth "tongues" of water and horizon lines and keeper holes. There were several guides down below the Cribworks with ropes acting as safety. I was feeling pretty relaxed at this point. It really was a blast and I pride myself in being a very strong swimmer, so I was just awed and excited about the power of the water surging through the cribs.

We all got back in the raft and Tom spun us out of the eddy. We were grabbed by the fierce current and went flying down the angry foam. But about half way through the cribs, the raft inexplicably stood upright in a hole and we flipped over. I felt myself being pulled under and then shot down the rapids at what felt like 100 miles an hour. I was struggling to get oriented, and when I finally did pop up above the surface, I only saw an unnatural blue light. I realized I was *underneath* the capsized raft and was still being flushed down the river with it. The power and the roar of the water was overwhelming. There was a small air pocket under the raft, but every time I tried to catch a breath, the current would bounce it and I would get a mouthful of water.

It took only seconds of terrorized flailing for air for me to register how bad this really could get. My brain did a semi-profound, "Ruh-roh…I could be in deep shit here."

Then I was pulled under again, deep this time. I felt my knees banging against rocks. The blue light was gone. Then I felt someone tugging at me. When I popped to the surface, I saw Tom's panicked blue eyes as large as saucers.

What does one say at a time like this? "Thanks, honey! Can I buy you a beer?" (Later I would find out that the guides secretly called me "Queen of Cribworking" as a snarky reference to Tom's and my age difference.)

**Guiding on the West Branch of the Penobscot River, 1995.
(Note the gold wedding band still on his finger)**

That night, as we sat outside the guide loft in Tom's beat-up old black Ford pickup truck drinking beer, he said to me, "I don't ever want to lose you. Not since I just found you again."

He took off the gold wedding band that he wore on his pinky finger and he slipped it on my ring finger. It fit perfectly. He said, "This ring belonged to my Pepe, and it means the world to me. Will you wear it? Will you be my wife?"

I have never taken that ring off in all these years. Not ever.

Postscript: Carol Leonard and Tom Lajoie have been together for twenty-three years. They were officially married ten years after the original proposal, on the summit of Mt. Cadillac at sunrise thirteen years ago... although Tom says it feels more like a hundred and thirteen.

FIRST LIGHT ~ This is with our wedding officiant, Peter Roy, Esquire, Ellsworth attorney extraordinaire...it was very sweet.

THE ROAD IN

Mud and Muck and Mosquitoes and Mildew = Miserable

When Tom and I had been together for ten years, we bought a parcel of land situated on a wild river in Ellsworth, Maine where we thought we would build our homestead. But, as fate and a tenacious realtor named Casper would have it, we ended up with a "smokin' hot deal" a year later: a 400-acre tract of wilderness across the road from our original piece. This land had been a cattle farm in the early 1900s, no remaining structures, but a large, still-cleared hay field, forests, streams, and three (encroaching) beaver flowages/trout ponds. We named the land Bad Beaver Farm.

Tom and I made a pact that we would be mindful stewards of this land and be as respectful of our gift as humanly possible. In the summer of 2006, we put in a road to reach the field where we planned to build our permanent home. We slogged through the mud, chain-sawed the trees, cut lengths for firewood, brought up Tom's huge, old Mobark chipper, chipped all the brush, reeked of gasoline, fought off black flies and mosquitoes the size of small pigeons. We slept in smelly, mildewed clothes. Even our dogs permanently stank of stagnant vernal pools.

When we first trailered up Tom's Mobark 290 industrial-sized wood-chipper from NH, we were a little south of Portland when it blew a tire. KA*POW!* We pulled to the side of I-95 and Tom got out to inspect the damage and said the rim was "junk"; it was now too dented to be able to install a spare tire. He jacked it up to remove the damaged rim. This made me *very* nervous, as it had rained so heavily the previous week that the shoulder was too soft to support the jack, and the chipper kept wobbling ominously over my husband's unsuspecting body as he crouched on the downhill side of the behemoth.

I don't usually interfere with Tommy World—but I couldn't tolerate this potential for disaster. I said, "Tom! This is unsafe. You gotta figure out a better way."

Tom rummaged around in the back of his pickup and came back with a long strip of aluminum grating that he was planning to use at the camp as a rain-splash diverter/boot scraper in the deck in front of the entry door. He put this underneath the jack to stabilize it and prevented it from sinking in the quicksand. This worked like a dream, although the grate was too dented after this episode to be used as originally intended—if and *when* we ever got a deck.

It was now 4:45 on a Friday evening, and we had to look for a new rim for an industrial-sized machine. We drove to the nearest town and found a tire store franchise. They were getting ready to close for the weekend, so they were not incredibly psyched to see us pull in with a funky custom-smashed rim.

The first scruffy looking, bleary-eyed guy to look at the rim said, "Nah. We got nuthin' that'd fit this lug-nut pattern."

Tom was not about to quit now. "Do you have your inventory computerized?"

The guy rolled his eyes. I knew he was just dying to get out of there and have a 12 pack and a shot of Jack.

"Yeah. Why?"

Tom flipped through the bolt patterns until he found one that had the matching 5-bolt pattern he was looking for. It was from a 1967 Chrysler Imperial. "This will do it."

The guy looked at us like we were perfectly nuts but we left the franchise with the perfect rim and tire—or so we thought.

When we got back to the crippled Mobark, Tom was again crouched underneath the swaying machine as huge tractor-trailers zoomed by on I-95. Every time a semi-truck blasted by, it created a vacuum of turbulent air that made the Mobark tip precariously. *ZOOM! Tip. ZOOM! Tip. ZOOM! Topple...squish.* I was pushed to the limit of my tolerance.

Tom finally got the new/vintage Chrysler rim on the Mobark, but the offset was not right; it rubbed against the spring shackles of the chipper. (This, by the way, is just what Tom told me—I had no idea what in the hell he was talking about). At this point, it was getting dark and I was thinking that we should start heading to the Comfort Inn in Portland for the night. That and a shot of Jack sounded incredibly appealing to me.

But...Tom just flipped the rim around and put it on backwards and all five bolts lined up. All fantasies about the Comfort Inn were gone. Then Tom said that the center hub of the rim was too small for the Mobark. The Comfort Inn's lure returned for a split second before he remembered that he had a cordless Sawzall in the back of the truck—with three charged batteries (of course he did).

Tom sawed and hacked and sawed through the life of all three batteries until the center hub fit perfectly. We were on our way to Ellsworth after only a four-hour delay.

That same custom rim is on the Mobark today.

Sometimes I think I am too old for this stuff.

Sawzalling on I-95

We were putting a road in through a thick forest to the field, which was about a half a mile from the main road. It was a typical Maine forest of mixed trees—hardwoods and softwoods. It was thick with downed spruce and tall pine and "popple" (this is what Mainers call poplar), and lovely mossy glens with vernal pools. Tom chain-sawed the trees down and cut the trunks to stove length for firewood. I dragged the treetops and brush and fed them to the jaws of the Mobark, which spewed out mountains of evergreen smelling chips. We later used the chips for landscaping.

Tom is amazing with a chainsaw. I swear I'd let him shave my legs with it. He studied each tree to decide where he wanted it to fall, then made the perfect cuts as though he were cutting through butter, and the tree would fall crashing down exactly where he planned. I think Tom is part beaver.

We worked on the road on weekends all summer. Tom's father, Leo Lajoie and his brother, Lee Lajoie came up to help us a great deal of the time. Unfortunately for the four of us, it rained *a lot* that summer. The road soon turned into a quagmire of mud and muck and deep ruts of sludge that came up to the running boards of the truck. Tom hauled up some huge wooden timbers that his friend AJ got from a job building a Concord Hospital expansion. These were timbers that had been in our front field at home, that I had been bitching about as just too white-trashy for words. But now I was growing to appreciate all the crap that Tom constantly dragged home from jobs. All that redneck hoarding was starting to prove useful. Tom and his dad threw the timbers in the muck and the planks disappeared from sight pretty quickly, but we were able to drive over them and not get stuck.

The rain also brought hoards of flying insects, a veritable plague of bloodthirsty bugs of biblical proportion. First came the black flies, then B-52 bomber mosquitoes—and just when we thought we could handle the annoyance and pain came the most ferocious of them all, the deer flies. Tom made me wear a logging safety helmet with a mesh face-guard and ear protection when I was working feeding the chipper. The flies would get up under the face-guard and bite mercilessly all around the perimeter of the helmet. Any exposed skin was chewed and covered in little bloody speckles that itched like hell. The only time they didn't attack was when the chipper was running. Something about the huge noise and/or vibration from the Mobark made them stay away, one weird benefit from feeding the beast.

When the road was about halfway to the field, all progress came to a screeching halt…temporarily. Tom was using a peavey pike to try to pry out a large log that was stuck in the roller-blades of the chipper. Somehow the peavey slipped and sheared through the gas line. The chipper was hemorrhaging gas all over the ground—spewing out gallons of precious fluid. Tom told me to stick my finger in the tubing while he whittled a stick that would fit the diameter to stanch the leaking fuel. I was lying in the pine needles with a torrent of gas running down my arm.

Good thing I don't smoke.

Tom got the gas line plugged enough for us to go look for parts to fix it. We drove around to several auto parts stores in Ellsworth while he picked up all the widgets he needed to create a fuel-shutoff valve. I stayed in the truck because I smelled like a cocktail of gasoline mixed with the tantalizing aromas of sweat and mildew.

He finally got all the pieces he needed and went back and installed the homemade fuel shutoff valve, and the old Mobark was fixed and we were back in business.

I honestly don't know how Tom knows how to do all the stuff that he can do.

The baddest dam beaver of them all.

By the end of summer, we finally got the road cleared all the way to the field, but there was one last remaining tree that needed to go, out at the entrance to our drive. It was on the tarred road, the old "Bangor Road." Tom was studying it. I knew it was leaning in the wrong direction as it was growing out of the side of the road bank. Tom doesn't usually screw up—but I had a bad feeling about this tree.

He handed me a long metal pole and told me to push the tree away from the road when he made his cut. I looked up at this huge tree, and I was standing there poking it with a measly, pathetic toothpick. I felt like Don Quixote jousting with the windmill. As soon as Tom made the uphill cut, it twisted and started coming right at me.

I screamed, "I can't push it!"

Tom ran over to me and tried to push it back, just as the tree fell forward and hit the top live wire—the "hot wire" of the road's electric lines. A huge jolt of electricity surged through the tree and into our bodies.

ZZAAAAAPPP! (I swear my hair has been wicked curly ever since. Is this possible?)

Then the tree bounced down onto the next wire, the neutral line and stopped dead. The tree was leaning up against the electrical lines in the middle of the road. Tom managed to drop the tree and get it cut up before anyone in authority meandered down the road.

I was just standing there with my mouth dropped open, still zinging from the shock. I guess even beavers occasionally make mistakes.

Tom asked, "Honey, is your life insurance policy paid up?"

My hair has been amazingly curly ever since. I'm serious.

The road we put in to Bad Beaver!

LAST CALL FOR THE COMFORT INN

Tom's old 1972 400B LULL

I guess it's become clear to me by now that I'm never going to get to lounge in bed with Tom at the Comfort Inn, enjoying an adult beverage and watching old movies while various and sundry pieces of his equipment get repaired. Tom is way too clever for that to ever happen. Rats.

After much discussion, we decided we would start building our fishing cabin, Camp Kwitchabitchin – hidden in a lovely copse of trees, an old oak grove/wind break – in the middle of our field. This site pulled me like a magnet, so I was incredibly excited about this. Tom had salvaged, for free, a dozen huge 24' long engineered wood beams that were also unattractive denizens of our front field in NH. He borrowed a 24' long wooden flatbed trailer from another builder to bring the beams to Ellsworth for our foundation.

A great quote from Tom at the time: "The first lesson in borrowing is to never do it. Because if they lent it to you, it's probably junk, and guaranteed you're going to break it."

As we were heading up the highway Downeast, we noticed intermittent black marks on the road following us. When we switched lanes, the black marks switched lanes too. Tom swore under his breath and pulled over.

He found that the frame of the trailer was rusted out and couldn't support the tremendous weight of the beams. The spring shackles had smashed through the frame (there are those damn shackles again!) The plywood bed of the trailer was riding on the tire.

We shifted the load. Let me tell you, this was not easy to do, but we got the beams shifted to the other side of the bed to take the weight off the damaged side. We got about twenty minutes down the road before a car pulled up beside us with people waving frantically and pointing at the tire. I only saw a lot of black smoke.

The friction from the rubbing tire had caught the plywood on fire and the tire was beginning to melt. Tom grabbed a beer out of the cooler and put the fire out. I could tell he was some upset to needlessly waste a perfectly good beer like this. I was certain that this time we would finally make it to the Comfort Inn. I was already deciding what I was going to order from Room Service.

Then Tom said he had a cordless Skilsaw in the back of the truck with a charged battery (of course he did). He cut a rectangular notch out of the plywood trailer bed for the tire to spin in unhampered. And off we went.

He did do this. Seriously, I could not make this stuff up if I tried.

Engineering the foundation beams

THE BUILDING OF CAMP KWITCHABITCHIN

Cunnin' cabin shingled with Tom's homemade shingles from our own cedar trees. All materials were found, scrounged, gifted—and Re-Purposed!

So far at Bad Beaver we have built the most cunnin' cabin that we have named Camp Kwitchabitchin. We decided to build the cabin first. (Well, actually, it started out as a screen house and then morphed into a 22×24×20-foot-high structure—my fault entirely.) Our pact with each other was that it had to be constructed with ***no out-of-pocket money.*** It had to be built entirely with salvaged materials that we had scrounged or hauled back from the dump for the last twelve years. Fortunately, Tom is a builder — and a pack rat (he says he is a "collector"). All the stuff he had piled in our front field at home in New Hampshire, that I had complained about for years as being too white trashy for words, was now found gold.

Once we finally got our road to the field, we had it graveled with gravel from our land (there are many glacial gravel deposits scattered throughout the forests). We seeded the banks of the drive with conservation mix. That very fall the deer and moose grazed every single clover plant to the ground.

First we brought in electricity. Yes, there was a minuscule discussion about being off the grid. I lived off the grid for several years in the late Sixties, so I really don't have a driving ambition to recreate that lifestyle, unless forced to by current political idiocy. We hired Buddy, an independent hydroelectric contractor (everyone up here in Downeast Maine is named either "Bud" or "Buddy"). The poles were wired to the entrance to the field where Tom and I put the remaining electric underground. We dug a trench with an excavator, slogged through the rain and clay and breathed in toxic fumes, gluing the PVC conduit together. Tom blew the string for the lines through 350 ft. of conduit with a leaf blower!

Tom wiring the conjugal bushing for our electric service

We excavated 6 holes for pre-cast cement pilings. (Note: No live trees were downed in this project. The cabin is built in the midst of some magnificent oaks, one of which is literally rubbing on the west fascia, much to Tom's consternation, but I wouldn't let him cut it down.) Tom had already trucked up his old 1972 LULL to the land, so it was a cinch to lift the beams and set them in place. Tom's father, Leo, a highway engineer, helped tremendously in this phase of the project, in the placement of the foundation beams.

The beams were too long, but before Tom could saw them off, I said, "Honey, this looks kinda small — couldn't we just cantilever a screen porch over the east side overlooking the pond?" Yup. Now the cabin had grown exponentially.

Because the cabin footprint had now increased by 8 feet, the gable ends also grew (amazing how that happens). Now it was 20 feet to the ridge beam — so of course this allowed for a second story sleeping loft *and* the new screened porch. We placed plywood on the deck and I got busy applying my mechanical drafting skills, acquired in a Design/Build course that I had taken at Yestermorrow School in Vermont so I'd be able to design our permanent house articulately enough for Tom to build it.

I arranged all the window sashes that we had hauled up in the most pleasing, light-conscious design possible, painted them all deep green — and basically left it up to Tom to build the frames and make it all work.

Here's how we "re-purposed" the windows:

On the south-facing gable is the front entrance. The front doors are vintage French double doors that Tom dragged home from the Hopkinton dump. These doors have two sidelights that I rescued from my brother David's barn before he moved away. This entryway gets great wintertime sun and solar gain. Up in the open gable is a mullioned antique diamond-paned glass window that came from Saint John the Divine Catholic cathedral in Lowell, MA.

The south gable, sleeping loft's Catholic window

On the west side (driveway side) is a mullioned 9 over 6 paned window mooched from our forester's barn, left over from when he retrofitted his house. This is next to the wood stove. In the "kitchen area" (I have this in quotations because at this point in our process we didn't have running water — yet), supposedly the well was going in the next week, but when I asked (yet another) Buddy-the-well-driller if he was still on schedule, he replied, "Prub-ly." Above where the kitchen sink is theoretically going to be are two ganged double hung windows from Tom's parents' barn of unknown origin.

On the north-facing gable is a huge double casement window that Tom salvaged from a job. On one side is a smaller casement that came out of a New Hampshire neighbor's bathroom. We couldn't find a match for the other side for the longest time, until one day Tom found the perfect casement in a dumpster. Up in the sleeping loft are two double-hungs, nondescript, but they provide great cross ventilation. The sleeping loft windows are in the tops of the trees.

On the east side (beaver pond side) are two very large paned windows that I also reclaimed from my brother's barn. Since these are in the cantilevered porch, Tom hinged them awning-style and they swing out and hook up via a pulley system. Also on this side are vintage double doors that open onto the side porch. These doors have tremendous sentimental value. They came out of Tom's parent's farmhouse where the boys grew up; probably these were the original doors. The house was a classic New Englander where the front door opened directly to the stairway to the second floor. In the winter, when the four brothers were young, they would open those double doors, position themselves at the top of the stairs on their flying saucers, fly down the stairs, out the front door and across the lawn on the snow.

The side porch at Camp Kwitchabitchin overlooking the beaver pond (before the exterior was finished with Tom's shingles)

As I have said, I left it to Tom to figure out the framing part. He is a true genius. He framed all the walls on the deck and then raised them up with pump wall jacks. I have to admit that the 2×4s were store bought. The way I squared that was I emptied out Tom's change drawer that he had emptied his pants pockets into after work for the past twelve years. The change weighed 140 pounds. I put it in a rolling suitcase and rolled it up the handicap ramp at the bank. The bank tellers looked delirious to see me coming. Some of it I had to bring home to wash in the dishwasher because it was too disgusting with gunked-up sawdust. Guess how much 140 pounds of change comes to? $1,500.00. That covered the cost of all the 2×4s and then some. (Like the cute acorn exterior light fixtures I found at Lowe's.)

Tom made fast friends with our forester, Dave Warren of Surry. Dave knows a tremendous amount about the Maine forests. He also had stacks and stacks of sawn lumber from our local woods in his back field. Tom finagled a deal with Dave to exchange the boards for our cabin in return for installing Dave and Jeannie's new kitchen and bathroom. It worked out swell. We covered the frame with Dave's funky pine boards before the walls were jacked up. Tom taught me how to use an air nail-gun. At first I had lots of "shiners," but soon I was keeping up with the best of them. To temporarily finish it off, Tom covered all the walls with a weatherproof "rain-jacket" material that really does keep the elements out, even in the dead of winter.

I didn't care much for the pump jacking up of the gable ends. It made me squirrelly nervous. The whole structure wobbled ominously when it got about half way up. Tom said to keep jacking for godsake, so I just closed my eyes, took a deep breath and trusted him that the whole damn thing wasn't going to come crashing down and squash us like June bugs. Once the walls were erect Tom braced them with twist-outs. When the last gable was up, Tom put a small fir at the peak for good luck.

**Tom and Carol's cousin, Al Homstead of
Surry, pump jacking up the east side**

We were only able to work on our cabin on weekends. Tom's left-hand man from his construction crew in NH, Liam "Casey" O'Brien, came up to Bad Beaver to help with the roof — thank god. I never could have done it. The ridgepole is a huge 10×16×24' long composite beam that had been sitting outside, marinating, in our field for a couple of years. It was swollen with moisture, so it must've weighed about 1000 pounds. There is a fabulous oak tree smack in front of the cabin, directly in the way, so the LULL was of no help here.

Tom put a bowing plank across from the sleeping loft to the Catholic window and was trying to slide the ridge beam across to the notch in the gable end. I was down below taking pictures and praying. Casey was at the other gable/loft end, when the beam fell and hit Casey. Judas Priest! I had visions of Casey permanently in a wheelchair. Casey is a quick, wiry guy, an avid rock climber. Somehow he managed to twist out of the way of the crashing behemoth, the beam only just grazing his left shoulder.

Tom doesn't usually miscalculate but this is an accident waiting to happen. Here is Tom with the killer beam that almost took Casey out, minutes before it fell (Casey is at the other end)

I thought at this point we would go to Plan B, but noooo, those two kept right at it. No stinking, 1000 -pound beam was going to outsmart *them*. Tom tied a rope around the beam, threw it over the gable end, and told me to go outside and hold the rope. I said if the beam fell again and I was holding this stupid measly rope, it would catapult me into the beaver pond. In retrospect, I think Tom thought all the screaming was not helpful.

Tom and Casey after the near miss

Because I was banished to the outside, I never did get to see how those two managed to get the beam in place, but they did. There it sits, comfortably in its notches. I see it overhead, first thing when I open my eyes every morning—the killer beam that almost took out Casey. I have a great photo of the two of them afterward, sitting on the porch drinking a beer, looking totally exhausted.

The behemoth ridge beam currently snug in place

Tom and Casey managed to get the entire roof done in one weekend. They worked like dogs. They got the roof rafters in place, then we covered those with more of Dave's funky pine boards.

Dave would stand there watching and would say about a particularly wide board, "That's a Civil War pine right there, by Jesus."

Casey was outside with a skillsaw, cutting the boards to length. Tom was balanced up on the roof rafters air-nailing the boards in place. I was running in between the two of them, from Casey cutting, up a ladder to the sleeping loft, handing the boards up to Tom on the roof, then scrambling back down the ladder again to Casey. Every damn board. By the end of the day my thighs and arm muscles were screaming/burning. I was about to complain when I looked up at Tom miserably sweating buckets in the blazing sun. I decided to keep my pain to myself.

We placed a great louvered cupola with a curved verdigris copper roof that Tom brought back from a job as a crown on the new roof. I had an old copper ram weather vane kicking around the house (I did, honest). He, Hector the Protector, is now up there pointing out the direction of the wind with his butt. It is cunnin'.

Miraculously, Tom still has all of his fingers…so far. He bought a turn-of-the-century Maine SHINGLE MILL to make our own shingles from the cedar trees on our land. The intention was to sheath all the exterior walls with homemade cedar shingles. The only problem I saw with this plan is that the shingle mill itself looks like a Dickinsonian nightmare way to lose several digits. Huge maniacally spinning blades. No guards. There was a telling sign on the mill when Tom purchased it. It says:

NO SMOKING
NO DRINKING
NO F*CKING AROUND IN GENERAL

Let me digress a little bit here and give you the back-story of when Tom bought the shingle mill. We drove to In-The-Middle-Of-Nowhere, Maine to meet with the older gentleman who had advertised his mill in Uncle Henry's. I learned that his name was Milan Lake (pronounced MY-lan). This surprised me, as "Milan" is an old family name of mine, it's an uncommon Maine Irish potato-digger name. Milan Leonard was my great-great-grandfather and I have his yellowing, Union discharge papers from the Civil War. Milan is also the name of my son.

My curiosity was piqued. I asked, "How did your parents come up with the name 'Milan?'"

At which point, Mr. Lake paused and looked at me with pity, having already surmised that I was riding the short bus. Then he said, very slowly, "Well, I don't know, deah. That happened before I was bawn."

My Redneck Life #2 – Tom's 19th-century Maine shingle mill

But Tom did keep all his fingers intact; he was flying digit free. He assembled and ran that mill like a champ. He cut more than enough shingles to securely clad our little cabin in fragrant, sweet smelling cedar from our forest. Now that the camp was weather tight, we could move our focus indoors. I painted the floor a sage green from some leftover paint I had in the cellar. Tom's brother, Lee — who is an electrical engineer — spent a weekend with us wiring the cabin. They decided to use metal clad cable instead of the standard Romex. This cable gives the exposed wiring a wonderful vintage look of an old fire hazard hunting camp. As a surprise, Lee wired a great rustic wrought iron twigs and leaves chandelier over our dining space.

Tom built "cupboard stairs" up to the sleeping loft. They are just steep enough to allow our two dogs to be able to make it up to bed with us. We put a railing up in the loft that came from a deck that Tom renovated. I capped that with a fabulous antique newel post that I had liberated from a friend's barn in New Hampshire many years ago. Tom installed an old refurbished ceiling fan he had junking around in his shop. Mostly now that fan blows the heat from the wood stove down from the sleeping loft where it gets to be about 110 degrees.

All appliances and furnishings are second-hand/hand-me-downs from sympathetic relatives and friends. The best score was some ratty overstuffed furniture, a couch and two hugely fat overstuffed chairs that my sister-in-law was throwing out. I re-covered them with sophisticated slipcovers and now they look impressive. My mom gave us a "cabin warming" present of a beautiful rug with fish and squirrels, acorns and pine cones. Actually, everyone got into the spirit and commitment to cheapness—sometimes to a fault. Tom and I found we had to politely refuse a lot of pure junk gleaned from people's cellars and barns.

Looking down from the original sleeping loft

But the end result is adorable. I *love* our little cabin! I am totally, madly in love with it. We're still uncertain about the design of the real house, but we'll spend time in the cabin to get used to the cycles of the sun for solar gain and the seasons and the weather. Tom has already dynamited and cleared the space for the barn (35' x 70'), so apparently that's next. It is all very exciting.

150-year-old white cedar root burl

This is the "brain" of the cabin. Tom found this 150-year-old white cedar root burl in one of our swamps near a landing. He hauled it out with his LULL and trimmed off the roots. We brought it home to NH and put it in the garage. All that winter, when we had a few moments to spare, we would sit in the garage enjoying a beverage and chat while we picked all the dirt and debris out of the brain's crevasses with lobster picks and toothbrushes. This burl is the hub of all the camp's activities.

LULA'S SINK

The kitchen at Camp Kwitchabitchin

I love my kitchen sink at camp. Several winters past, Tom and I were visiting our forester to see his new piece of land on a mountain in Holden. Up the mountainside was a dilapidated old shack that I went to investigate. The shack looked like at one time it had been cunnin'. It had little shelves over the windows for birds' nests and a rose arbor arching over the front door. Kids had obviously been partying in the place since it had been abandoned. It was full of trash and bottles and was ripped to shreds.

I poked around in the mess and realized that underneath some wet, decomposing, fallen plasterboard was not a dead animal but, in fact, was a moldy old mink stole—a woman had lived here! I found smashed, mismatched, floral china plates and delicate pink and white demitasse cups with the handles broken off. In a cardboard shoe box, I found the woman's personal effects. From an old black and white photo, a lovely dark haired woman smiled back. She was sitting on a rock by the ocean holding an alert looking wire haired terrier. I found canceled check stubs dated 1973. Her name was Lula Cram.

How had she ended up here in this desolate place? Did she live here alone? Why? What happened to her? Was she crazy? (Later, I Googled her name and found she died in 1999 at the age of 93 and was buried in the Millinocket cemetery.) I said to Tom that I wanted to know more about her pioneering spirit, and I wanted something of Lula's to remember her by. I looked around the hovel. The only thing that was still intact was Lula's huge old white porcelain cast iron sink, the kind of sink with a long drain board on one side. I cleaned some leaves and debris out of the sink to check its condition. Tom was eyeing me warily. I said I wanted Lula Cram's kitchen sink. Tom said that's what he was afraid I was going to say.

We got permission for the sink from our forester and we hiked back up the snowy trail to get it. The sink was still attached to the wall, but Tom managed to free it with brute strength. It weighed at least 200 pounds. Now the problem was how to get it down the mountain in the snow back to the truck. Tom had the great idea that we would simply slide the sink down the mountainside. He pushed it with his foot and the thing took off like a toboggan, careening completely out of control. Tom and I went running down the hill in the snow after it, shouting *"STOP!"* at the sink. It came to rest in a snow bank about six inches away from the passenger side door of Tom's new white pickup truck.

Thank god. Tom would've been wicked mad at me.

Lula's sink after a little Comet and elbow grease

We had an artesian well drilled in the dead of winter, probably the coldest day possible, around the end of February. Well-driller Buddy Gilbert from Ellsworth was very professional and somehow got his rig in from the long way, as our front driveway had a ten-foot high ice and snow bank plowed in front of it, courtesy of the Ellsworth Highway Dept. It was many degrees below freezing, so the guys all stood around drinking coffee and hopping from one foot to the other to stay warm, while the rig drilled. They went down 110 feet and got decent water, so Mr. Gilbert and company were gone by noontime, leaving behind a tsunami of gray silt.

That spring, Tom borrowed an excavator and dug a six-foot deep trench below the frost line from our new artesian well to the camp. Then he decided while he was at it, he would dig a gray water system for the camp's new kitchen sink. (Of course he did.)

Unfortunately, the rubble from this trench was about six feet high and looked like hell. Honestly, it looked like a bomb had gone off in our front

41

yard, so I was crabby. I left to go clean our other cottage in Surry and when I got back, not only had Tom filled it all back in—he covered the scar with wood chips from our Mobark chipper, so it looked fabulously landscaped.

That man has such unbelievable survival instincts.

Tom put in a frost-free farm hydrant so we could have running water all year round. He hooked this up under the camp to a gas water heater and pressure tank that someone had given him, cast off from a job. How he knows how to do all this stuff, I will never know, but I'm not complaining. I could hear him under the camp swearing as he bumped around down there. He had copper pipe fittings and propane torches and plastic tubing and myriad gizmos all over the side porch, but in the end, I had hot and cold running water to my reclaimed kitchen sink!

My husband knocks my socks off.

THE OUTHOUSE ~ KWITCHAPISSIN

The outhouse at Bad Beaver ~ Kwitchapissin

I told Tom that I was getting just too damn old to keep digging holes in the woods anymore, especially in the middle of winter, literally freezing my butt off. Finally, after a lot of pitiful nagging on my part, Tom finagled an excavator and we commenced building the most awesome Shat Shack.

First, we sited the outhouse. We agreed the only place it could possibly go was to the north of the camp. The east side is too low and potentially wet, the south side is where our (real) house is going to be someday and the west side would be in the driveway, so not much discussion there.

Tom dug a very deep hole in the woods with the borrowed excavator. We have some terrific banks of gravel on our land and Tom nailed one in his excavation for the new Pooporium. Perfect for drainage. Over this he placed a crib he'd made out of pressure treated 6 x 6's that he had left marinating in the field. The foundation of the structure is 4 ½' wide x 7' long. He built up from there. I have to tell you right here that Tom sawed all the boards for the outhouse from our own trees with his portable sawmill. He really did. I know this makes him sound like a seriously manic overachiever, but what else can I say? Truly, I get exhausted just writing about this, but he sawed the lumber from our downed pine and popple trees in the morning—and the boards were on the outhouse that afternoon.

He made the seat of the throne from flawless, pure white popple. I found a gorgeous red oak toilet seat and the end result would make any Home & Garden crapper jealous. (Here is a "Note from Things I Have Learned the Hard Way Department": We now have a hook on the wall behind the wood stove where this lovely oak toilet seat resides in the winter. What I learned that first winter was that when the temperature is hovering around zero and you park your delicate derriere in the hoar frost on the seat, your bum freezes to the wood and it feels like your skin is ripping off when you stand up. Now, we can just grab the seat on the go when we dash out the door and then we have a yummy, warm throne to perch on. Brilliant!)

Ah, but here's the rub: Immediately after completing the one-holah, Tom announced that he was going to do the honors of trying it out for size. Alrighty then, go for it. Almost immediately after this, however, Tom dropped his measuring tape down into the hole.

We looked at each other in disbelief. Who does this? I told him he was definitely on his own with this one.

Personally, I would have gone to EBS to buy a new measuring tape. But, noooo, he had to retrieve the tape. He took a steel rake and tried to lean down into the Loo to scoop it out, but it was too deep. He enlisted my help. I held onto his belt loops while he dangled in, his legs flailing in the air as he fished around in the depths. I asked him if he wanted me to send in the oxygen.

He got it, though. He held up his tape measure proudly. I told him he had to put his initials on it with a permanent marker because I never wanted to touch it by mistake.

Interior of the Pooporium with lace curtains

As I did before, I designed the placement of the windows and door—and left it to Tom to figure out how to frame it all. It goes like this [see photo]: There are two windows on either side of the structure. The windows came from a 1920's lake house in NH that was torn down to make way for a McMansion. The door is a beautiful old solid wood door that I painted the deep dark green that I've used on all the trim. Tom decided to put a metal shed roof on the structure with a slight pitch to it for snow melt.

I found we had some shutters in a shed that fit the windows perfectly. I painted the shutters the same trim green and Tom put up a little plant shelf under the window that holds a crock planted by my mother. I found some elegant lace curtains in a thrift store that I washed and hung in the windows. The great thing about lace that I've discovered is that you can easily see out—but it's really quite difficult to see in. I love sitting on the throne looking out in the forest and watching the birds hopping around on the bird feeders in the trees.

The last thing about the outhouse that makes it so spectacular is kind of embarrassing, only because this makes me sound spoiled rotten. Tom and I were walking in the woods one day when we saw a huge boulder that had been cleft in half by a glacier. This left it with a beautiful enormous flat face. I said wouldn't this be a fabulous step for something? Yep. While I was in Ellsworth grocery shopping, Tom and his brother, Lee, picked the boulder up with the LULL and deposited it as near to the outhouse as they could get. Then they wrestled it in place in front of the door with steel rollers, I am not kidding. See, this does make me sound pathetically bratty, doesn't it? (As Tom says, "Pussy hair pulls a freight train.") Lastly, I planted perennial Lily-of-the-Valley that my sister had discarded, around the behemoth boulder and up along the path.

The final piece of plumbing that Tom did was, he put in an outdoor shower attached to the back of the cabin. This is a most excellent personal hygiene method, although I'm afraid it might get a tad nippy come October. But in September it is glorious. The days are crisp with brilliant sunshine. There is just a hint of chill in the air but the water is yummy-hot. I can stand on the wooden shower platform and look out over the field to the beaver flowage where the swamp maples have already turned prematurely red. A great blue heron flies overhead and squawks like a prehistoric Pterodactyl.

I am filled with gratitude for my life here—truly, it doesn't get any better than this.

The infamous "Pussy hair pulls a freight train" rock step

HOW THE NAME BAD BEAVER CAME TO BE

The New Masonic Lodge at Giardia Pond

We have bad beavers. Not only bad—we have *mason* beavers. When Tom and I first purchased our land in Ellsworth, a beaver dam was partially flooding the big main field that had once been a cattle pasture in the early 1900s. The field where we wanted to build our house. Now the east side of the field was under about two feet of water, complete with beautiful

Blue Flag irises. Tom said straight away that this was not acceptable; the beavers would have to go.

One of our rare marital spats ensued. I think I won, having drawn the line at mammalian violence. I said Tom would simply have to outsmart them—how hard could this be? I felt confident that Tom could outwit the world's second largest rodent.

The first time Tom messed with the dam, he only partially broke it down with his hands and feet, to make a sluice way to lower the water level. The water began gushing over the breach and the beaver pond/ex-little stream was lowered by about a foot and a half.

What we didn't know at the time is that the sound of gushing water drives beavers mad.

When we returned to the field the next day, we saw enormous "swales" dug through the field. Overnight, the angry beavers had dug *trenches* about two feet deep and three feet wide so they could float *WHOLE TREES* to repair their dam. Now the front of the dam resembled a log fortress, complete with a sentry beaver. I thought to myself, "Uh-oh, I think this means war."

Tom, not to be out-done by this engineering marvel *and* not having rodent incisor teeth, resorted to his trusty Husqvarna. He got busy with his chainsaw and removed a whole front section of the dam. Now the water was rushing out at a tremendous rate. We could tell by the damp rings on the skeletal dead trees in the pond that the water was lower by around two feet.

"That should fix the little buggers," said Tom confidently.

When we returned a few days later, our mouths dropped open in absolute shock. The beavers had repaired the dam with *ROCKS!* They swam on their backs carrying rocks the size of melons on their chests—then they mortared the rocks in with *clay*. The whole dam resembled the Tower of London. We had Mason Beavers!

Apparently, only a small, aberrant branch of the beaver family has this rare, double-recessive gene to employ masonry.

Now we had to resort to some serious ingenuity—so we Googled "beaver removal". First Tom got the plans for a "Beaver Deceiver" which he installed immediately. This was a wooden sluice-like contraption he made that had thick wire mesh on the underside, the theory being that the beavers can't figure out how to dam something upside down. Right-O. This did deceive them for about two whole weeks (which, incidentally, is the longest time anything has worked).

Next came the "Beaver Baffler" which was some kind of elbowed-PVC gizmo with holes drilled along the sides. We can't even find that anymore—we have no idea what the beavers did with it. They hid it somewhere.

And so the contest between wonderful man and intelligent rodent continues to this day. I did notice this spring that it looks like the beaver lodge has a second story addition—and a couple of new flower boxes out front.

Postscript: I wrote this almost seven years ago when I was still quite beaver naïve. Now I know that WE WILL NEVER WIN. The beavers have now flooded over 50 acres of prime real estate. The gloves are off. The next batch of those effing rodents is going to be residing *in my freezer.*

**Early morning view of the beaver flowage
from the side porch at Bad Beaver**

Gladys Tries to Kill Me

Gladys laughing

Tom got up before the crack of dawn to go saw lumber. I just don't know why this man cannot sleep in. He's got some kind of infernal-internal alarm clock that makes him start fidgeting and getting antsy if he is in bed after 5:00 AM. Not me, Lovey, there's nothing I like more than luxuriating in bed at camp with Mossy Oak camouflage flannel sheets and a down comforter, reading the *Bangor Daily News* with a steaming cup of Earl Grey tea with milk and honey.

I am in the loft at the Beeve with our two black mutts, Phaedra and Gladys. All of a sudden, Gladys makes a frustrated sound that sounds eerily like ChewBacca. She is at the top of the steep cupboard stairs and she is furious. Gladys has gone to work every day with Tom for fourteen years. She doesn't understand why Tom is leaving her behind these days. She doesn't realize that she is getting too old to brave the elements the way she used to, that in her senior years, she doesn't thermo-regulate well at all.

She glares at me. She is clearly angry. Gladys is Tom's first and only dog and he is profoundly attached to her. Don't get me wrong, I don't feel competitive with her. She's been with us since she was eight weeks old. I *adore* Gladys. I just think it is sad that she can't accompany Tom all the time on the job any more.

I say, "All right, Gladys, I'll take you down the stairs so you can go to work." (Tom has been *carrying her* down the stairs, which I simply cannot do because she weighs about seventy pounds.)

I start at the top of the stairs—which have no sidewalls—and I hold onto her collar to coax her down. We get only *two stairs down* before her hind end gives out and she slides sideways. She slides and I fall over the side of the stairs—in slow motion—floating through the air about ten feet up with Gladys following after me. I watch this as though detached.

I land on my back in front of the sink in the kitchen. Gladys lands squarely on top of me. I swear I hear Gladys laugh. She looks at me as though this has been great fun—I have been her own personal airbag. She shakes it off and gets up to go to work. I, on the other hand, think I have a stress fracture in my right heel. I check every bone in my body. I can put weight on my heel, even though it hurts like hell, so I guess I've been lucky and it's only bruised.

Two days later, there is a lovely cedar sidewall along the staircase enclosing it in from the kitchen. I thank Tom for building it.

He says, "No problem. I was really worried about Gladys."

I shoot him a look that would stop a freight train. You know… sometimes I honestly don't know if Tom deliberately says stuff like this so he'll have to sleep alone for the next six months.

OUR GERIATRIC GIRRRLS

Phaedra and Gladys on the beach in Surry

Tom and I have been together long enough now that the pets that we acquired in the early bloom of our relationship have all become noble senior citizens. We have two dogs and two cats and not one is younger than an octogenarian. Lately, I've been feeling like we are running a nursing home for four-legged assisted living.

Tom's dog, Gladys, is 15 (that's 105 in dog years). She seems fine, although she occasionally has dizzy spells, is stone deaf and is blind in one eye. But her will is as enthusiastic as when she was a puppy—it's just that the body doesn't follow suit so well these days. Gladys is Tom's first and only dog. She went to work with him on construction sites every day for fourteen years.

Gladys has occasional gastrointestinal issues—which causes her to shit upstairs in a back bedroom at night. I've gone through about fifty throw rugs. We found that if we don't feed her commercial dog food she is much better. I'm not sure what kind of cancerous mystery meat they're putting in canned dog food, but it literally disturbs the crap out of her. Now we feed her an old lady's dinner of canned pumpkin and cottage cheese and saltines at night and she is fine. In the morning we cook her a breakfast of boiled white rice and green beans and ground turkey. A dog's breakfast—fit for a queen. I swear I spend more time cooking for Gladys than I do for us.

My dog, Phaedra, is probably around 13—she was a found pound hound so I'm not sure exactly how old she is. She's been a great dog but recently she started having horrific seizures, really terrifying to watch— long minutes of paddling and snapping at the air, screaming and peeing herself. When she comes out of the seizures, she doesn't recognize us for a while. It is assumed that she has a brain tumor that is causing swelling. I was going to put her down, but my vet, whom I adore, put her on Prednisone and Phenobarbital, and she seems stable on that. Actually, yesterday she was running around playing with a stick like she was a puppy again.

The downside to these medications is that they make Phay incredibly thirsty, and she drinks copious amounts of water. They also make her incontinent, so she is leaking like an old Chevy. I spend my days running around with towels, wiping up pools of urine on the floor where she's been sleeping. We've rolled up all the rugs. Do they make doggie Depends?

The house smells like my old friend Dow after he'd been on a month long bender. I don't know how long I can hang with this.

Gladys and Phaedra are both large black mixed breeds. They weigh between 70 and 80 pounds, so getting them in and out of cars has become a struggle. Tom can lift them easily, but I have to create kind of a ramp deal to get them in. I am getting a good workout by dead-lifting these be-atches. I have also started giving them a daily massage.

We have a mean old alley cat named Tabouli. My son brought her home from Manhattan 17 years ago. She is probably the nastiest, snarliest cat ever born. She is also now about the size of a hassock. She's a calico cat, white with large black and brown splotches. From behind, she looks like a giant soccer ball. If she's pissed off, she will randomly approach a dog and hiss and smack her in the face for no apparent reason. She is ill tempered and absolutely miserable—and she's lucky she's still alive. I'm just too afraid of her to try to get her in a carrier to bring her to the vet.

The last time I brought Tabouli to the vet for a check-up was many years ago, because it was a true nightmare. First, I put her in a cardboard cat carrier. I don't know what I was thinking. Tabouli shredded her way through the cardboard before I was even out the door. She made mincemeat out of that measly carrier. The only thing I had at the time to carry her in was a large picnic cooler. I put her in the cooler and brought her to the vet for her shots. At the animal hospital, she was pounding on the top of the cooler so violently that I had to put my foot on the top to keep her from smashing her way out. I was standing on the cooler as people recoiled in horror as to what could possibly be making such a snarling, hissing, growling racket inside a picnic cooler.

Finally, a timid elderly woman spoke up for everyone in the room, "Do you mind my asking what you've got in there?"

I responded gravely, "Tasmanian Devil."

Everyone shifted to the other side of the waiting room.

Tom says Tabouli needs a long walk with Doctor Remington. I think she needs Kevorkian Therapy.

Tabouli lives on the third floor, which is accessed by a steel spiral staircase. She is so heavy now that when she goes up and down it sounds like an elephant is stomping on the metal stairs. I've recently changed her name to Catzilla.

Our other cat, Shrimpy, is a pretty cool cat. Shrimpy is the "youngster" of the bunch, being only 81 in human years. She was foisted off on me as a kitten by a friend who claimed that Shrimpy was a descendant of calico cats kept by a crazy, famous cat lady/artist in Nova Scotia.

Shrimpy is a great huntress, and goes in and out of the house from a window that we leave ajar for her, because the window opens onto the second floor roof system. The only problem with this arrangement is that the window is right over the headboard of our bed, so there is a lot of traffic in and out, directly over Tom's head.

This winter, when the window was closed, Shrimpy would try to pry it open with her claw in the middle of the night. This was not conducive to sleep. One night while she was picking at the window, I may have sort of batted at her to get her to stop. She jumped down and landed on Tom's sleeping face. I could feel Tom radiating sheer fury. He was seething.

"Did Shrimpy just scratch you?" I asked as I turned on the light.

Tom turned to me. Boy Howdy! Did she ever. He had eight bleeding puncture wounds on his face. He looked like a bloody pincushion.

It was at this moment that I heard Shrimpy heave and gack up a partially digested mouse under our bed.

Even though this geriatric care for ancient animals has become a royal P.I.T.A., we love our girls. Tom and I both know the specter of the "Youth in Asia" decision is looming mightily. It's definitely coming sooner rather than later. I just hope that we can make this decision in a timely manner. I do not want them to suffer. I want them to be comfortable in their final days. In this perspective, all the cooking and cleaning and massaging just seems like payback for all those years of unconditional love and companionship from them. I know we don't have much time left.

I guess Dow didn't really smell that bad after all. I can hang with it.

MY DOG CROSSED OVER TODAY

Elderly Phaedra and Carol on the cranberry flats on Graham Lake

I woke in a cold sweat because I heard Phaedra screaming downstairs. I threw off the covers and jumped out of bed and started running to the stairs.

Tom asked, "What?"

"Phaedra's having a seizure!"

Tom was right behind me, barreling down the stairs.

Our thirteen-year-old mixed black Lab was on her dog bed in the family room, in a full-blown seizure. She'd had a couple of episodes a month ago; our vet assumed she had a brain tumor that was causing swelling. He put her on Phenobarbital to suppress seizure activity, and that had worked—until now. It was unbelievably horrific to watch our dog in the throes of this struggle, frantic paddling with her legs and snapping at the air, screaming and pissing herself. Now she was stiff and arching her neck and lunging on her side.

Tom said gently, "You've got to pull the plug on this, Carol."

"I know. I know. I will. But we can't move her right now, she's too sick."

Tom and I put our hands on Phay and talked to her gently as she thrashed around. It's such a helpless feeling. Previously, she had come out of the seizure after only a few minutes and then it was a while before she recognized us. Now it seemed like it was going on...and on...and on. Many, *many* minutes went by as Phay screamed, sending spittle flying. All we could do was gently keep our hands on her to let her know that we were there. I kept thinking she would eventually come out of it like before.

This was not meant to be.

What she did do was, when she recovered enough to be able to walk— she started marching. Manically marching, around and around the room, circling the perimeter, panting anxiously. Around and around, a hundred times. Tom sat down on the daybed. I tried to hold Phay to get her to stop but she would break free and keep marching, rubbing against the outer walls.

I said, "Oh my god, this is like *The Yellow Wallpaper*."

"Only worse," Tom said.

Every so often, during one of her loops, I would hold up a bowl of water and she would drink thirstily. After several rounds of water, she squatted down and peed what seemed like a gallon of urine. Phay's eyes flew open in fear that she was going to be reprimanded, but I smiled at her and gave her permission to do whatever she needed to do. It was only an oriental rug—it could be cleaned.

Finally, after what seemed like hours, Phay started to get tired and I got her to lie down on her bed. She was still panting anxiously. I started to massage her and this seemed to begin to calm her down. I dimmed the lights way down low. I heard a gentle snore and looked up to see that Tom had fallen asleep. He was too long for the daybed so his legs were hanging over the end, but he was fast asleep.

I rolled up in a blanket and lay down next to Phay and started massaging her hind end. She seemed to really enjoy this and she kept moving her butt toward me to get a better angle for the massage. I knew I was lying in urine and her fur that was shedding. As I rubbed her, fur was sticking to my urine-soaked arms, but I didn't care at this point. I just kept thinking she'd come out of it.

As her labored breathing eased a little bit, I was at her head and Phay laid her white muzzle on my chest. She looked me square in the eyes and she raised both eyebrows. I knew what she was saying to me. My throat was almost too tight to speak, but I did.

"Okay, Phay, I know it's time to let you go. You've been a *great* dog. I remember when Kudra and I brought you home from the pound. You were so afraid of people that you wouldn't get in the car—do you remember that? Now being in the car is your favorite thing in the whole world. But that day, you tried to strong-arm us; you wouldn't bend your legs. Kudra and I had to lift you—stiff-legged—into the back seat, and you rode the whole way home standing straight up. And then you didn't know how to go up stairs. Wow, that was a long time ago, Phay."

Phay closed her eyes and started to rest. I must have dozed off with my hand on her shoulder. That's when I felt the first jolt. It felt like 1000 volts of electricity jolted through Phay's body.

"Phay, *NO!*"

This time her screams were agonizing. Tom jumped up.

"We are out of here!" he yelled. Somehow, he grabbed Phay in her whole bed and carried her to the door. I ran ahead of him and opened the back hatch of the Jeep, and he placed her in the back. I flattened the seats so I could be with her. Somehow, our other dog, our fifteen-year-old Newfy mutt, Gladys, was standing beside the car. Tom scooped Gladys up and put her in the front passenger seat and we were racing to the emergency veterinary clinic.

I was riding backwards as we transported Phay to the hospital. I was holding her as she thrashed. She just would not give up. I kept talking to her softly, telling her it wasn't going to be long now. Every so often I would stick my head up and see the route backwards, St. Paul's School, Concord Hospital, Concord High School. This made me dizzy so I only looked down and stroked Phay. *HURRY!*

Tom called CAVES on the way to tell them we were coming in. It was 6:00 AM. When we got there a vet and a vet tech were waiting with a stretcher. They took Phay away to sedate her with IV Valium and left Tom and me to sign the euthanasia consent. Tom and I sat numbly waiting in the waiting room. We were staring straight ahead, holding hands. Tom said he felt liked he'd been hit by a bus.

The vet tech took us to a side room and then they wheeled in Phay. She was pretty out of it but I know she recognized us. The vet asked if we wanted more time. I said, "No." The vet skillfully injected two syringes of blue liquid and Phay was gone. They wheeled Phay back to the car and put her in the back. She looked like she was sleeping. Gladys saw Phay and her eyes got huge. She definitely knew that Phay wasn't "sleeping."

We drove the long way home. Tom had big silent tears rolling down his cheeks. When we got to the Long Pond reservoir, we pulled over to the side of the road. The sun had risen and it was a glorious spring morning with the early light sparkling on the water. I laced my fingers in Tom's calloused hand and we sat quietly grieving as the morning unfolded.

Postscript:

Phaedra died on Easter Sunday, April 2012. Tom's dog, Gladys died a year later, May 2013. They were true and loyal friends to the end of their days.

The pet cemetery at Bad Beaver

HIGH HEELS AND HEADLAMPS

For many years, one of the items on my bucket list has been to observe the spring midnight mating frenzy of the ever-elusive Spotted Salamander— *Ambystoma masculatum*. I've heard about this legendary event but have never had the privilege of witnessing it in the flesh, so to speak. I say "ever-elusive" because about the only time the spotted salamanders come up from their subterranean existence is for one night in the spring when they return to their natal vernal pools – pools of spring melt water – to perform their secretive annual mating ritual. These pools are temporary, so predator fish are absent and the salamanders can breed in safety.

This year I was determined to be a salamander voyeur. I asked my friend, Dave Anderson, who is a naturalist and Director of Education for the Society for the Protection of New Hampshire Forests, how to tell when the "Big Night" was about to happen. Dave is a veritable encyclopedia of natural history phenomena, especially when it pertains to lusty mating habits and procreation.

Here's how Dave explained what to look for: "It is the first overnight rain when temperatures remain above 42 degrees. The salamanders only move under the cover of darkness, and they migrate en masse to their ancestral vernal pools. They remain there for mating purposes but need rain in order to migrate back to the woods. Obviously, rain or lack thereof, and intermittent freezing and thawing, can disrupt their migration. The males typically arrive first, just like wood frogs. A really good proxy for when to pay close attention is when you hear the very first spring peeper calls—the earliest single spring peeper. Also, when you hear the wood frogs by day—like quacking ducks in vernal pools."

Dave continued with his directions: "Salamanders make no vocalizations (even during mating!) They hide beneath leaf litter each day. The only way to watch their slimy dance is with a flashlight and going out to a vernal pool on a rainy night often called "the big night"—you'd feel the same if you only mated once a year. Males attend females while wafting pheromones with their tails and nudging the often-larger females to go down to the bottom of the pool to collect a few sperm packets called "spermatophores" from the bottom. It's an amazing backyard ritual that few people ever see because you have to go out in the cold April rain with a flashlight and stand at a vernal pool in the dark woods. That's a hell of a commitment."

Now I was more determined than ever to invade the salamanders' sexual privacy. On April 10, I was on Long Pond road near the town reservoir pulling the last of my traps out for the end of beaver trapping season, when I heard a cacophony of "quacking" coming from deep in the woods. I followed the racket until I came to a large, beautiful vernal pool full of wood frogs calling and cavorting on the surface of the water. I just knew this would be the perfect place for the slithery Rite of Spring.

That night there was a light rain, more like a drizzle really, but it had been such a dry spring that I was afraid I was going to miss the show. I dragged Tom out there at 10:00 PM anyway. I bribed him by packing up some snacks and a jug of cheap vino. We trooped through the dark woods but when we got there…nuthin…nada…dit-squat. We were met by an eerie silence. No movement in the water either—not a frog-quack to be heard.

I was so disappointed. I was beginning to think this whole orgiastic event was a figment of some bio-porn writer's lusty imagination. I gave up on seeing the magical dancing salamanders until next year.

A couple of nights later, Tom and I went out to dinner at The Gaslighter in Concord. When we exited the restaurant, it was pouring rain—an unexpected torrential downpour. Driving home, frogs were crossing the roads en masse and, unfortunately, there were dozens of squished frog bodies littered everywhere.

I said to Tom, "Oh my god, tonight is the *'Big Night!'*"

Because I wasn't counting on this and we had been out dining, I had on very high heels (of course I did). But we did happen to have two headlamps in the car, so we headed back to the same vernal pool. I stumbled through the dank woods in my stilettos, trying desperately not to break my ankle. As I hobbled up to the far side of the pool...there they were! Shining in our headlamps in the leaves in the bottom of the pool were the ever elusive, horny salamanders. There were dozens of writhing balls of spiraling salamanders weaving in and out and around each other. I couldn't believe how excited I was. What an honor. This was the nuts!

I watched, mesmerized, at the courtship dance driven solely by odor. The salamanders themselves looked beautiful and glistening in the flashlights. They were about six inches long, jet black with bright yellow spots running along their sides. They began by rubbing their chins together gently and then circled each other on the bottom of the pond, placing their heads under each other's tail as they spun around and around. The male then climbed on the female's back and repeatedly rubbed his chin against her. Then he would try to lure her away by wiggling the tip of his tail enticingly—thus apparently wafting the pheromones—to direct her to his spermatophore. How unbelievably sexy is that? In this dreamy state, they spiraled around and around each other, dancing in total silence.

I was in awe. What is it about this dance that is so soulful? I think there's something about the pheromone lust, gentle chin rubbing, spiraling slow dance in the ancestral pool that reminds one about the cycles of the seasons, the emergence of Spring and fertility and rebirth and the wonder of life itself.

I looked over at Tom who was squatting next to me, shining his headlamp beam into the pool, enjoying the show immensely. What other man in the world would put up with my insanity like this? What a gift he is.

He said, "Looking for love in all the right places."

Tom plucked a mystical, spinning salamander out of the pool and placed it gently in my hand.

I said, "Coitus interruptus" and let my smooth amphibian go back to his date.

Ah. But what was this? Did I just get a waft of human pheromones?

I leaned over and began rubbing my chin seductively against Tom's shoulder.

He grinned at me with rain dripping off his nose. He said, "Let's go home."

BUCKET LIST # 13 ~ CHECK!

SUMMER

BEAVERGATE!

This gate was made by Tom and his friend, Leroy Bragdon of Brownsville, Maine for our 5th wedding anniversary. Tom told me to draw my "fantasy gate", so I did. I drew it out on large cardboard; it has beavers and cattails and twigs. Tom cut out my drawing and traced it onto steel. Tom and Leroy cut the entire gate out of sheet metal with acetylene torches, welded it up and galvanized it. The gate is 28 feet long and weighs 500 pounds. It is spectacular. Tom and his brother Lee and their dad, Leo, installed the gate at Bad Beaver in July, 2010. Then Carol painted it red—which pissed all the men off.

THE OWL ON THE HIGHWAY

I was bone tired. All I wanted to do was get back to my friend's house where I had been staying, have a glass of wine and then crawl into bed for a couple of days. I had been up for almost 24 hours now, catching babies at the maternity hospital where I had been moonlighting in Rumford, Maine. There had just been an unprecedented tsunami of births, which I assumed must be the aftermath of the autumnal Full Moon.

It was dusk and I could barely keep my eyes open as I drove down Route 2 back to Bethel to my friend's warm and cozy home. As I drove, a tractor-trailer going in the opposite direction passed a large pile of feathers in the middle of the highway and whipped up a huge wing that signaled to me. Splayed barred feathers with an enormous wingspan. I slammed on my brakes.

That was an *owl's* wing!

I pulled over to the side of the highway and ran to the middle of the road. In the midst of the pile of feathers, a head with enormous brown eyes looked up at me. Oh my god, it's a large barred owl and it's still alive! The owl blinked and continued to stare at me. He must have been hit when he was after some road kill. Tractor-trailers were screaming by us on both lanes of the highway. I had to get him out of there. One wing was bent at an unnatural angle behind his body. I squatted down and gently righted the wing to lie close to his body again. I scooped up the whole bird and ran back to my car.

I assumed the owl was in shock and in the process of dying because he just continued to stare calmly, looking deep into my eyes with his ridiculously huge black eyes. He looked so serene. My heart was breaking for him. I rocked him gently and talked to him softly as I waited for his light to go out. He continued to look directly at me. After about ten minutes of this, I thought maybe he was still in shock and getting cold, so I sat in the driver's seat and turned on the heat in my car. After some more minutes of being scrutinized by those liquid brown eyes, I decided to drive him to my friend's house.

I called my friend, who was also a midwife, and told her to get her two daughters together to see this magnificent bird and to dim the lights and put her dog outside. I drove to Bethel still cradling the owl in my arms. I decided to name him Ovid.

I brought Ovid into my friend's house where her daughters gently stroked his beautiful barred feathers and talked softly to him. I realized what a wonderful gift it was to be in the presence of such a powerful raptor. The girls were delighted. After some more time passed, Ovid was still very much alive. I said I guess we should bring him to the local vet to be checked out.

The local vet was a little vexed because it was after hours and he was planning on going home. He was talking too loudly for a dying bird, his energy was all wrong. He took Ovid from me, a bit roughly in my opinion, and proceeded to twist Ovid's neck around, to see if his neck was broken, I assumed. Ovid did not like this vet one bit. Silently, and with the speed of light, Ovid pierced through the fatty palm of the vet's hand with his razor sharp talon, clean through to the other side. I was astounded, but I also think the vet deserved this because he was so insensitive.

The vet hissed at me under his breath, "Get the damn talon out of my hand."

The talon was like a thick, curved darning needle that had just effortlessly pierced through some semi-soft cheese. I pressed the pointed end of the talon that was sticking out of the vet's flesh and it popped out backwards, a clean puncture wound all the way through. Ovid retracted his foot.

The vet was furious. I grinned at Ovid.

I said, "Give me that owl." I grabbed Ovid and held him safely in my arms, turning my body away from the vet.

The vet pointed to a large cardboard box in the corner. He said I could put the owl in there overnight until someone from his office could drive the owl to a raptor rehabilitator in the morning. I declined his offer. I didn't want this powerful creature humiliated like that.

I conned my friend into driving me to the raptor rehabilitator, even though it was an hour away and it was getting late. She and I gossiped about all the scandals at the hospital, what doctor was sleeping with which nurse, etc, the entire way to the raptor center. I held Ovid in my arms, lightly stroking his lovely barred feathers. The whole time he was gazing up at me with those saucer-sized round brown eyes.

My friend said, "That owl looks like he's in love with you."

"I'm sure he's just in shock," I replied.

We got to the raptor center, which was really a trailer in the middle of nowhere in Norway, Maine with a lot of cages outside. The rehabilitator was expecting us. I walked in holding Ovid and the owl expert's eyes got pretty huge as well.

She said, "Hold on a minute." She went to a drawer and put on some long, heavy-duty leather falconer's gloves.

She grasped hold of Ovid around his legs and snapped him free from me. Ovid, as if waking from a dream, rose up to his full majesty and unfurled his wings and let out a scream, his beak huge and yellow. I could see his tongue. I fell backward from the compression of his four-foot wingspan pounding the air around him. *Jesus!*

Ovid hadn't been in shock at all. He'd been mesmerized.

The owl lady said, "This bird could have ripped your face off. It could have been a disaster driving with him in your car like that. But, birds like this can also tell when someone is kind. He knew you were helping him. He could tell you weren't afraid of him, so he allowed you to care for him."

I knew then that Ovid had given me the gift of being able to protect him. I will truly treasure and dream about those bottomless brown eyes trusting me, for the rest of my life.

Fortunately, Ovid's wing was not broken, only badly sprained. He stayed at the raptor center, recuperating, for three months. I got a letter with photographs of him being released back into the wild. My heart soared as I saw his big barred body and enormous wing span effortlessly gliding over the tops of pine trees to freedom.

**Ovid the Owl and Carol with the raptor
rehabilitator in Norway, Maine.**

IMUS IN THE MORNING

Our first rooster was a turken. A turken isn't really a cross between a turkey and a chicken—it's all chicken. It's just that it has a naked neck so it looks like a turkey. In other words, it's incredibly ugly. Our first rooster was also a mistake. We had ordered a couple dozen "hardy brown egg laying mix" chicks from McMurray Hatchery that came in the mail from Iowa on Easter morning. The US Postal Service in Manchester actually called us on Easter Sunday and waited for us to come get our chicks. Bless their softy government-employee hearts. I think they must've been having some kind of Easter epiphany—that or they didn't want to be responsible for a peeping baby chick's demise on their watch. All the fuzzy chicks arrived safe and sound—just really thirsty. The mix included one "exotic" chick that ended up being a male turken.

At first I thought that maybe all the other chicks were pecking the feathers out of this poor little one's neck. It looked so bare and wrinkled and vulnerable—kind of scrotal. This chick with the bare neck also had a topknot of yellow feathers that stuck straight up on top of its head—so when he pecked, he looked like a fantasy bird from a Dr. Seuss book. Soon it became pretty evident that this guy was growing bigger and stronger and bossier than all the rest.

As he matured, his feathers were a beautiful golden color with long curved tail feathers, but his damn neck was impossible to ignore. It was

76

so scrawny and scaly…he looked like a train wreck. Hence, he was named Imus, and he developed the same sexist attitude as his namesake.

In the beginning, Imus was a pretty reasonable chap, leading and protecting his beautiful free-range flock of multi-colored girls. Reasonable, that is, until the big "Chicken Holocaust of '99," when he snapped and literally lost his mind. A dog from down the road, a huge brutish Chow named Tony, came into our yard when we weren't home and killed 17 of our girls for sport. Apparently, Imus fought to save them but he was no match for Tony. Carnage and feathers were everywhere. A neighbor, Mr. O'Boyle, sadly brought a wheelbarrow full of carcasses from his lawn. We were devastated. So was Imus. I'm sure Imus felt like he had failed in his duty to protect his harem. He was never the same after that. He went batshit crazy.

I, on the other hand, was furious. I called the local animal control officer, and he read me the rules about protecting domestic livestock from predators. I called Tony's owner and told him if his Chow was ever in our yard again—I was going to shoot him. I meant it. We never saw that dog again.

But the damage was done. Imus became a ferocious lunatic who would launch a vicious attack when he thought the hens were being threatened. Unfortunately, that included *us*. It became almost impossible to go into the coop to feed them. I had to approach the coop with a garbage can lid like a shield and a hockey stick to fend off Imus, who would fly at me, razor-sharp spurs first. It became a nightmare chore to deal with him.

The deciding event was when Imus attacked a little boy who was visiting my birth center. That was just too much. Short of sending Imus to a chicken therapist and putting him on Prozac, I had no idea what to do with him. So I decided to foist him off on my good friend Kendall. Why she agreed to take him in, I'll never know, but she did. I put on leather fireplace gloves and threw a towel over Imus when he was sleeping, and drove him to Kendall's in the middle of the night.

Kendall's coop was a funky structure that had a metal roof under a high window. Somehow, Imus discovered how to escape out the window every morning and slide down the metal roof to the yard below. It was a pretty amazing sight to see this big, awkward bird sliding on his back with his feet sticking straight out in front of him, his bare neck arched forward, the whole way down to freedom.

Imus was lucky. He got to spend several more years in this world as a solitary bird until one day he never returned from roaming.

What I learned from Imus is that roosters take their role as flock champion very, *very* seriously.

ARMAND THE GOOD

Our second rooster was an impossibly handsome Columbian Wyandotte. This rooster had a rose-comb and beautiful long, curved tail feathers that were black and green iridescent in the sun. He was a big boy and he knew he was gorgeous. He proudly strutted his stuff. This rooster, Armand, was friendly and very polite—but he was also insanely horny. Even though Armand had a couple dozen "girlfriends" to entertain him, he was insatiable. He was very considerate and gentle though; he never ripped up the girls like some other clodhopper roosters do. He always did this little two-step, sideways shuffle-mating dance with one wing fanned out to impress a girl and get her in his orbit before he mounted her. This was his idea of sexy chicken foreplay, I guess.

One time early in Armand's mating career, a nice conservative neighbor from down the road was visiting. This older gentleman and I were standing on the lawn chatting when Armand came over and mounted a hen at the man's feet. Armand banged the snot out of her right there. When Armand was finished, the hen straightened up and shook her feathers indignantly and stomped away.

The neighbor's mouth was dropped open. He said, "Did he just...? Jesus."

He shook his head and went home.

After a couple of years, Armand developed a mild respiratory affliction that occasionally made it hard for him to crow. It kind of seemed like a severe sore throat. I accidentally found a cure one night when I had

Armand in the living room in front of the wood stove to see if heat would help. I was drinking Scotch. Armand walked over and took a beak full. He sneezed and took another beak full. The next morning, he crowed like hell. Every once in a while I think he was faking a sore throat just so he would be invited in for a cocktail. Armand was the only Scotch-drinking rooster I ever heard of.

Armand also fathered the only chick ever to be hatched on our farm. This lack of hatchlings was probably more my fault than Armand's, as he was definitely hitting the mark. I just couldn't leave the fertilized eggs alone. Not trusting Nature to take Her course, I was always messing with them; so the one chick that hatched was a total surprise.

One night after Tom and I returned home from dining out, we both went in the coop to say goodnight to the ladies and gentleman. It was actually unusual for us to both be in the coop at the same time. I picked up one of the broody white Silkies that was setting on a clutch of eggs—and there was a fuzzy yellow golf-ball with two tiny black eyes looking back at us. She looked as astonished as we did.

Tom laughed, "Well, one actually made it despite your help."

"Oh my god, this is the cutest thing I've ever seen in my life," I sighed.

I named her "Winona" which means "first-born."

I sat for a couple of hours watching them, and I had the unbelievable good fortune to see the mother Silkie teach Winona how to eat. The mother picked up a kernel of cracked corn; dropped it in front of the baby and then peck...peck...pecked it and swallowed it. Winona just stood there watching. The mother repeated her lesson, although this time she *peck...peck...pecked* a little more empathically. Winona still didn't move. This time the mother hen took the corn and in frustration *PECK... PECK...PECKED!* pounding until Winona hopped over and pecked it and swallowed it. I swear I saw the mother hen roll her eyes as if to say, "We got a real live wire in this one."

Armand had an illustrious career that would have made any Casanova proud. He died one night in the dead of winter. I went into the coop in the morning and found him lying stiff and cold on the floor. I was immeasurably sad that I hadn't realized he was so gravely ill.

Maybe his death could have been prevented if only I had invited my old friend in for a nightcap.

LEWIS AND CLARK

A French woman who had a baby born at my birth center gave me her whole flock of Bantam chicks because she had to suddenly move out of state. The chicks were a great addition, except when they matured; we discovered that most of them were roosters. I already had Armand at the time, and I didn't want to cause any unrest in a perfectly contented flock... so I tried to give the fledgling roosters away. Nobody, but *nobody*, wanted a pack of testosterone driven, fowl tempered, teenaged male chickens.

It got to the point where they began challenging Armand's dominance, as he was an aging rock star by then. I couldn't stand the fighting. I decided to drive them deep into the woods and let them go to support the local wildlife. I know this sounds cruel, but my neighbors who are farmers do this all the time. I let all the fuzzy-footed boys go, with a prayer that their demise would be swift and painless.

About four days later, I couldn't believe what I saw. Two of the young Banty roosters had somehow made it back to the chicken yard. This means they had crossed a major stream, gone up and over a good-sized hill in the forest, and down a very long, overgrown field to get home. Because of their obvious excellent navigational skills, I named them Lewis and Clark.

Lewis could fly, and he wouldn't stay in the coop at night. He would fly up into a tree and roost there instead of in the hen house. I told him this was a pretty precarious habit, really not conducive to life, but he refused shelter. I was right. One morning, I saw a trail of brown feathers going down the driveway and I knew Lewis was gone.

Clark, however, wasn't going anywhere. He knew a good thing when he saw it. By now Armand was departed and Clark became the new king of the roost. He was very short and had a nasty temper. I think Clark had Napoleon's "short man syndrome." Seriously, he was mean to the girls because they were much bigger than he was. In short, Clark was a little bastard.

People told me Banty roosters could be fierce, and Clark was no exception. He raked all the hens' backs with his spurs when he mated with them until their backs were bloody and featherless. He was jealous of the big hens and made them cower in the corner to avoid his vicious attacks.

It all culminated one day when I went into the chicken yard and Blackie, a huge black Australorp, came running to me and jumped in my arms for help. Her eye was hanging out by the stalk. Clark had gouged out her eye in a jealous rage. That was the last straw. I decided right then that I was not turning a blind eye to this domestic violence situation any longer.

I asked Tom if he would help me kill Clark. We had never done this before, but Tom set up a log chopping block and got his ax. I held Clark's neck over the block and Tom took one swift chop, and Clark's head was on the ground. Here's where I made a mistake. I let go of Clark's body. He began flying crazily all around the yard in a frenzied zigzag pattern. Headless. It was quite unnerving.

Tom said, "Holy Fa%ck!...it really is true."

I buried Clark behind the compost pile but I didn't have any remorse. He was a terrible example of male macho chicken shit. Good riddance.

The next morning, when I opened my front door, I screamed to see Clark's head lying on the doormat.

The dogs had left me a trophy.

P. Diddy, Maine's Smallest Cock

I got our current rooster at the Davisville Flea Market. Please don't ask what possessed me. Obviously, I didn't know he was a *he* until some time later when he attempted his first crowing. His voice cracked like any other adolescent male, but he was *loud.*

This rooster is about the size of a healthy banana. Truly, I believe I may have Maine's smallest cock. But even in his mini state, he is a true stunner. P. Diddy is golden hued with blue and red feathers, almost like a small ornamental pheasant. He looks like an Aztec headdress shining in the sun. *Bling!*

Anyway, the girls absolutely *adore* P. Diddy. They follow him around and he finds juicy worms for them. He is the only rooster I've ever heard who actually *chuckles.* He makes sounds of pure delight when he finds a choice morsel for the girls. He always gives it to them first, at his expense. Such a suave gentleman. When they roost at night, P. Diddy is ensconced underneath the breasts of two of the largest hens, his little head sticking out from beneath their curvaceous, bodacious down feathers. If a rooster could smile deliriously, this'd be it.

P. Diddy is the Tom Cruise of the chicken kingdom. He's tiny for sure, but somehow, he knocks the ladies dead. They would follow him anywhere. When he crows, he puts his all into it. He stands on his tiptoes and throws his head back, and he almost falls over backwards every time he lets it rip.

But he gets the fertilizing job done. At first, I thought I might have to get him a stepladder or something—but nope. He is so fast and so on target, when he's done the hens look around like, "What was that breeze?"

One night last spring, P. Diddy was not in the roost at dusk. I didn't find him until the next morning when I heard a feeble attempt at a crow. I found him on his side in the back field, staggering and still trying to crow to alert the flock to danger. He had been beaten up very badly by a skunk and left for dead. I thought he was blind and brain damaged. His eyes were swollen shut and he couldn't stand or eat.

I brought him in the house and put him in the "Chicken Whisperer" which is a woven basket with a top that is warm and dark and safe. I fed him with an eyedropper for two weeks until he hobbled out of the basket to protect and be with his beloved girls once again. I swear they celebrated his return with the chicken equivalent of cheering; the noise of their joy at seeing him alive was deafening.

He made a complete recovery. Today he is running around on his fast little roadrunner legs making sure everyone is accounted for.

Long Live P. Diddy! He's the Man!

THE LOST TESTOSTERONE BOYS

Last spring, I bought twelve adorable baby chicks at the Davisville Flea market. They were advertised as Barred Rock and Golden Comet "pullets." I figured it would be good to have a small flock of new laying hens to get us through the winter. Tom was skeptical, and thought it was a mighty gamble to purchase our birds at the "Flea," but they looked healthy and well cared for to me. I brought them home and made the fuzzy little chicks comfy in our coop under the glowing red light of the mother heat-lamp.

This fall, as the hens got larger and *larger*, I kept looking for the first eggs in the nesting boxes. Nada. I marveled at how beautiful these hens were becoming, with extremely large, bright red combs and wattles...and flinty, shifty eyes. Surely, any day now, we would be rolling in tasty fresh eggs.

At the crack of dawn several weeks later, my eyes flew open as I was rudely awakened by a harsh sound. Then another one. Then another. A whole flock of jubilant voices raised in praise of another sunrise.

I said, "What the hell is that noise?"

Tom sighed. "It sounds like a gay men's chorus to me."

Yep. Every single one was a cock. They were dubbed The Lost Boys. When I complained bitterly about this to some other poultry people, I found that others had been bamboozled by the "pullet" vendor at the flea market as well. I was furious. If that guy is there next summer with his damn "pullets," I'm going to stand there with a sign that's says:

Beware! These chicks have dicks!

Now what was I going to do with all these boys? I stood in the chicken yard watching them pecking and scratching as I threw cracked corn to them. Another bunch of crack-heads. It was futile, I knew. We would never see our return on the cost of feed. I knew Tom was waiting for me to make a decision. I also knew it was just a matter of time before the testosterone kicked into high gear and they started fighting and flying at each other with lethal spurs first.

It was when I saw one of the boys actually *mount* another guy that I said, "That does it." I'm all for gay marriage and everything, but pretty soon these guys were going to start singing Judy Garland show tunes.

I called my friend and local farmer extraordinaire, Derek Owen, to help me out with this testosterone poisoning. Derek very kindly didn't laugh too hard when I explained my predicament. He agreed to show us how to process the birds for the freezer.

I got up early while it was still dark to try to catch the roosters while they were sleeping on their roost. I put on a headlamp and dragged two large dog kennels into the coop and snatched the first bird. He screamed bloody murder and alerted all his brothers that he had been abducted. Bedlam ensued. There was screaming and dust and feathers flying everywhere. Each bird fought and pounded his wings when I grabbed him. I was astounded at how heavy and strong they'd become. The biggest of The Lost Boys whipped around when I grabbed his leg and he knocked me down. I was lying on the coop floor with the wind knocked out of me. I was covered in chicken poop. Dammit! I chased him around until I got him in a corner and managed to nab him.

Tom was making coffee when I returned to the house.

"How'd it go?" he asked.

"Oh, fine." I said as I picked some feathers and shit out of my hair. "But I think somehow they knew the jig was up."

An hour later, we were at Derek's farm and he had everything prepared for us. He was so kind and funny and knowledgeable. Derek had large white mutton chop sideburns, so he looked for all the world like that old-fashioned guy on the Luden cough drops label.

Derek was wearing a ball cap that said, *"Farm Here to Eternity."*

This made me laugh because I had on a T-shirt that said, *"From Here to Maternity."*

The workroom in his barn was warm from the propane heater that was heating a large garbage barrel full of water. Derek handed me a long thermometer and told me to keep the water at 140 degrees. He and Tom went out to our truck to get the boys. I was wondering how I was going to fare with this plan, after all.

Attached to the wall was a funnel shaped metal cone, like an inverted highway marker cone. Derek showed Tom how to flip the bird upside down and stuff it down into the cone until its head stuck out of the bottom. Then he showed Tom how to feel for the jugular and stick a filet knife in the vein until the bird bled out into a bucket below. Watching the bird struggle made my stomach lurch and hurt my heart, so I didn't watch this part again. I said a little prayer for the protection of the spirit of the bird. I didn't let Tom know I was praying, though, because he seemed like he was doing just fine with this part.

Derek took the bird and dunked it into the hot water until the feathers came out easily by the handful. He hung the bird by one foot from the ceiling and I plucked out all the feathers into a garbage barrel below. This was surprisingly easy and the plucking went quickly. Derek said the hot water relaxed the muscles that held the feathers so they just peeled off. We got into a rhythm of Tom sticking and me plucking—until I realized that the birds' insides still needed to be cleaned out. I asked how that was done.

Derek grumbled, "I was wondering when you'd get around to that part."

Derek took his filet knife and cut off the head and showed me how to locate and remove the windpipe and esophagus from along side the neck. Then on the other end, he showed me how to insert the knife just below the anus and how to cut up in a "U" shape to avoid nicking the poop chute. Then using two fingers, how to go in and separate the fascia from the fat and remove the fat that is in a thick layer under the muscle. This was all very familiar to me somehow.

My hand entered the bird, which was incredibly warm and pliable from the hot water bath it had just had. I was astounded as my hand crept up into the bird and I could feel the intestines, the large, hard gizzard, the liver and kidney (chickens only have one kidney), and lastly the heart. I pulled gently, and all this came out in a slippery mass. I went back inside the bird and realized it felt delicious to me. I loved the way this felt.

Derek was watching this out of the corner of his eye. He said to Tom, "Oh good, the midwife's here."

Tom grinned at me. I know he was thankful that I was enjoying this—because he was looking a little skeeged out by this part himself. We were a good team. I knew we'd be able to do this in the future with meat birds, no problem.

As my hand traveled back inside the bird, searching the cavity, I located two large masses that felt about the size of Ping-Pong balls. I removed them and they were glistening, pure white orbs of remarkable beauty. There was the vas deferens.

Holy Rooster Balls! These nads were enormous!

Tom's mouth dropped open. "Jesus, those are almost the same size as mine."

"I know. I was thinking the same thing."

No wonder roosters were so macho. They just couldn't help it. It was their biological imperative.

Derek and Tom cleaned up the feathers and muck from the workroom while I cleaned the birds. I was thankful to Derek for his kindness and his expertise. Now we would have a dozen hefty cockerels in our freezer for the coming winter.

The next morning when I walked past the chicken coop, it was strangely silent. I felt a little sad. The silence made me nostalgic for just one more joyous chorus of "Somewhere Over the Rainbow."

YELLOW JACKET ANAPHYLAXIS

Today, I give thanks for my very life…literally. I came mere *minutes* from dying this summer. For once, I am not exaggerating.

On the last day of our summer vacation, I was walking back from the outhouse behind our cabin, Camp Kwitchabitchin, at Bad Beaver Farm when an angry stealth drone of an insect flew out from under the camp and stung me in the ankle. It burned like holy hell.

I said to Tom, "God! This *really* hurts!"

He rolled his eyes, "I don't know how you ever gave birth."

Weisenheimer. But his teasing ceased to be amusing when, ten minutes later, my lips swelled up and my hands and legs were numb and I became anxious and disoriented.

I said, "Honeeeey, I think I'm having an allergic reaction to this sting."

He said, "OK, we're all packed up and ready to go anyway. Let's go look for some Benadryl." So we hopped in the truck, intending to search for a pharmacy in downtown Ellsworth.

By the time we got to the end of our drive, however, and Tom got out to open the gate, I realized I was in MAJOR trouble—I was in true, full-blown anaphylactic shock. My throat was constricted, and I was suffocating. I couldn't talk to tell Tom what was happening, so I dialed 911. But when the dispatcher answered, I couldn't get any words out before I passed out and dropped the phone. Tom said later that when he got back to the truck; my eyes were rolled back in my skull. Tom frantically began driving like a bat out of hell to the hospital.

I was going in and out of consciousness. I was completely blind; all I could see was a searing white screen, even with my eyes open. Tom was yelling to the 911 dispatcher that he was going to blow through the traffic lights all the way up the hill on Main Street. Then he was yelling to me, "Stay with me! Stay with me!" I was sweating bullets. I started vomiting. Then I slid off the seat onto the floor.

A police car was waiting at the entrance to Maine Coast Memorial Hospital. Because we were pulling a long trailer, we had to park diagonally in the parking lot. Tom scooped me up off the floor and started running across the parking lot to the emergency room with me in his arms like a limp rag doll. He was screaming, "This is my wife! She's in anaphylactic shock!"

When I arrived in the triage room, my blood pressure was 69/35. I overheard the ER nurse say to the MD, "This woman is going south *fast*." I have never felt so crappy in all my life; all I could do was gasp for air. *Oh my god. Oh my god. Is this really it?* I truly thought it could be the end.

But then the ER people started shooting me up with every drug known to mankind for anaphylaxis—Epinephrine, Benadryl, Prednisone and a bunch of other stuff. In about ten minutes, my blazing white screen disappeared and I could see again. I started to rally. When I regained my vision, I looked over at a monitor and saw a blood pressure of 180/130.

Tom was standing next to my gurney. "Whose blood pressure is *that?*" I asked.

"Yours," he answered.

Holy Mother of God, that was close.

It happened again about three hours later when the drugs wore off. They told me it was called rebounding. Fortunately, I was still in the ER, so I got the same pharma cocktail all over again. At least there was no more airway swelling. This time I got unbelievable hives. I was covered with an angry red rash all over my body. I looked like I had the Bubonic Plague. Hives in between my toes. Hives in my ears, itchy as hell. Nasty raised purple welts on my face. I had hives on top of my hives. Because of the severity of my reaction, I had to stay the night in the ICU for observation.

But miraculously, by the next morning I was fine. This was a serious case of "better living through chemistry." The ER doctor came in to talk with me before I was discharged. We were discussing Tom's epic run across the parking lot—which was now, apparently, the talk of the hospital. How Tom folded me in his arms and *ran* with my dead weight of 160 lbs. How he ran with my limp rag doll body as if it was nothing. How he ran with me in his arms all the way to safety.

The ER doctor said if I had been alone, if Tom hadn't been there, I'd be dead. He said, "Your husband saved your life."

I told Tom I was never going to use the outhouse ever again. But the next day, Tom found the culprits: a hive of yellow jackets living in an old galvanized watering can underneath the camp. He swiftly dispatched them with some wasp killing spray. He checked under the whole rest of the camp to make sure there weren't any others. When he was sure it was safe, I went back to Camp Kwitchabitchin.

I was astounded to find that everything was the way it had been the day before. All was quiet. While I had been inches from the jaws of death, life went on its merry way at Bad Beaver. I sat under an oak tree, pleasant sunlight filtering through the leaves. A pileated woodpecker landed above me and started drumming for insects. Nothing had changed. Nothing, except that I now had a new appreciation for the insane capriciousness of life.

Much later, I had a conversation with a good friend of mine who is very interested in "near-death" experiences. He peppered me with questions, particularly about the brilliant blank white screen that I saw the entire time. Then he asked me if I thought I had a *choice* in the outcome. This question took me by surprise.

I considered this for a minute, but then I said, "No. I didn't get the sense that I had a 'choice' about whether I would go or whether I would stay. But what I absolutely *did* get was an extreme sense of well-being and calmness, that everything was going to be all right either way—so I wasn't committed to either outcome. I wasn't terrified. I just felt very trusting and loved and cared for the whole time."

But...I stayed. I was given the gift of life. I know that. I am a lucky woman and I lead a blessed existence, and for this I am truly grateful. I will savor every day to its fullest from now on.

"The Hounds from Hell are chasing me down,
but it ain't my time... it ain't my time."

My Vagina Saves My Life

DOCTOR FUN   17 May 2000

"We don't like the term 'beaver'. We feel that it's pejorative. We prefer to be called 'vagina squirrels'."

About a month after my brush with death, I had come to a clear understanding of how my body cleverly prevented me from dying during the anaphylactic episode. This realization caused me to write the following letter to the personable ER doctor who treated me:

Carol Leonard

Maine Coast Memorial Hospital
Ellsworth, Maine

Dear Dr. Maloney,

I don't know if you remember me or not—I was the midwife you saw last month in the ER of MCMH who was in the throes of severe anaphylactic shock from a yellow jacket sting. I know the following question may sound like a joke, but I'm actually quite serious:

Do you think it's possible that my vagina saved my life? When I was stung, the first thing that happened was that my vagina was burning and *ON FIRE!* I was stung in the ankle and within about 10 minutes, my vagina was screaming. Now, I'm thinking that the yellow jacket toxin was mainlined into my lymphatic system, which caused my vagina to immediately swell and constrict. In retrospect, had the sting been in my upper torso—it could have done the same thing to my *THROAT.* I never would have made it the 10 minutes to the hospital—or if I did, I certainly could've been brain damaged. (I did have mild throat involvement, in that my voice was very hoarse for the next couple of days, but I certainly didn't have airway obstruction like I might have, given the severity.)

Do you think my vagina took the hit for the team, so to speak?

Sincerely, Carol Leonard

To which I promptly got the following thoughtful and very professional response from the Family Practice doctor:

Hello Ms. Leonard,

I received your letter regarding your yellow jacket sting. I still think about your case as to how severe it was. I have no idea if your vagina saved you but it certainly reacted, as did the rest of your body. I do think having a sting on your leg bought you more time to reach the ER.

Hope all is well with you.

Frank Maloney, MD

Which, in turn, generated the following crème de la crème parody of his letter from an insanely funny midwife-friend of mine. She says:

I would have expected a reply like this:

Hello Ms. Leonard,

I received your letter regarding your bad beaver. I still think about your vagina and how swollen it was. Your vagina certainly saved you. It proves that even after menopause, your crotch can still give life. It was clearly well trained. I gotta get me one of those... I feel so vulnerable knowing I lack this cutting edge, life saving emergency equipment.

Hope all is well with you.

Fulla Baloney, MD

I sent this parody-reply to Dr. Maloney but I never heard back from him. When I told Tom that I had sent him this letter, he said, very seriously, "You better hope to hell that you never have to go back to that hospital in anaphylactic shock again. Because if you get this same doctor, that poor guy is going to *let you die.*"

MY SMELLY CANNAH

I have a wonderful, elderly woman, Mrs. Pinkham, who helps me clean my little seaside cottage every Saturday on Contention Cove in Surry. It's a bit hectic, because the turnover time between renters is only a couple of hours, so she is a godsend. Mrs. Pinkham is also adorable and is a wealth of pure Downeast wit.

One Saturday, we were rushing around doing last minute straightening-up. I think I was cleaning lobster juice off the top of the cook stove. Mrs. Pinkham came up to me and said very seriously, "Deah, your cannah smells really bad."

"Oh! I'm sorry." I discreetly twisted and scanned my backside to make sure I didn't have any offending, gnarly stuff on my butt.

What the heck is a "cannah?" Do I have a personal hygiene problem?

Mrs. Pinkham continued with her chore. But soon she came up to me again and said, "Your cannah is really stinky. It smells like low tide. I think we should do something about it."

I cruised stealthily into the bathroom and sniffed the toilet. Nope, not that either.

Mrs. Pinkham dusted some knick-knacks on the cupboard shelves while I wracked my brain, worrying about my nasty cannah.

Finally she said, "I think if we put some baking soda in it that will absorb the odah." She reached over and picked up the big black-enamel lobster pot that was draining on the sideboard.

Ah! The **canner.**

Thank you, dear Mrs. Pinkham. Yah can't can with a lobstah smellin' cannah, now can yah?

(Sorry…couldn't resist.)

MOMMY AS MUMMY

My 89-year-old mother, Louise Homstead Leonard McKinney, was showing some friends of hers our little camp at Bad Beaver when she fell and smashed her head against the wood stove. It was truly horrifying. She had a *huge* four-inch gash in her left temple. She kept saying, "I'm all right. I'm all right" as blood pooled everywhere. I was trying to assess how bad it was and whether we needed to go to the ER.

She claimed she had been trying to swat a mosquito on her knee. I said, "Mom, next time why don't you just let the mosquito bite you? It would be a hell of a lot cleaner."

We did end up in the Ellsworth Hospital ER. My mother had 10 staples in her temple, which fascinated me, so I was perversely taking pictures of her head with my cell phone. This aggravated her to no end. When they were done, my mom was all wrapped up with just her eyes peeking out. She looked like The Return of the Mummy. She looked so tiny and vulnerable lying there. My heart lurched as I thought, "What if this has long term consequences?" Then I thought, "Nah. She's a tough old bird. She's going to be fine."

Before we left, she complained to the ER nurse practitioner that her "tailbone" hurt. She dropped her shorts so the nurse could take a look at her bruised behind.

My mother turned to me and said sarcastically, "Oh, aren't you going to take a picture of this too?"

I said, "No, Mom, I don't want to terrify anyone."

On our way out, we passed through the ER waiting room. With her head wrapped in the huge bandage, my mom looked like the Revolutionary War guy in the famous fife and drum painting. The waiting room was packed with a couple dozen people, waiting miserably. They all looked at my mother in horror.

I pointed to my mother and said very loudly to the waiting room folks, "THIS IS WHAT HAPPENS WHEN YOU DRINK TOO MUCH."

The entire waiting room burst into laughter. My mother, who is a teatotaller, gave me a withering look. She was furious.

She hissed under her breath, "I can't believe you just said that! Now they're going to think I really had been drinking."

"Mom, there is not one person in that room who knows who you are."

"I don't care. That was not funny one bit. You are terrible. I just can't take you anywhere. Why did I ever let you out of your cage?"

And so on and so fawth. She reamed me out the whole way back to her cottage in Surry. But I was grinning the entire time. I love my mom. It was good and healthy to get her blood boiling again. It was totally worth it.

Postscript: Several days later my mother was checked out by a PA who told her that she had "a hole in her eardrum." My mom is going to physical therapy to improve her equilibrium. She *is* going to be just fine.

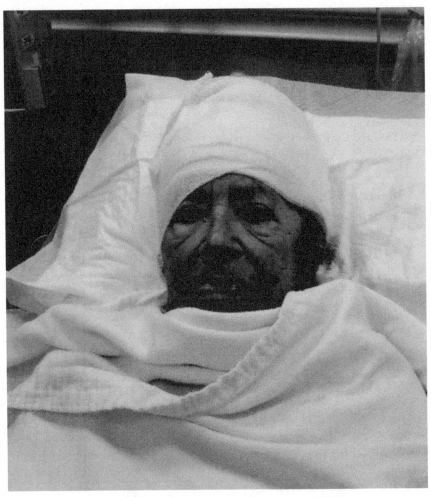

My mother in the ER–not happy (and YES,
absolutely, she is going to kill me.)

HULLOVA U-HAUL

Somehow it has become my job to re-register our little aluminum fishing boat so we can troll for mackerel on July 4th. The whole family is at our oceanfront cottage, "The SeaWitch" in Surry, and I want to fish mostly as a means of getting away from all the familiness that has started to suffocate me. Don't get me wrong, I *love* my in-laws; but after several days of being rained-in, in a small camp with everybody lolling around eating and drinking and then eating some more and listening to the Red Sox lose—even fishing sounds fabulous.

I bound up the steps to the Ellsworth City Hall where there are a few workmen replacing some granite stairs. All of a sudden I get the distinct feeling that my khaki skirt is way too short as I walk up above them. I tug my hem to see if I can cover another inch or two of exposed thigh. I look behind me, and sure enough, a worker averts his eyes away sideways. I want to yell, "Are you kidding me?!? I'm a flippin' Senior Citizen for gawd sake" as I huff and slam the heavy front door and enter the city offices.

I walk to the desk that registers boats, where I did the exact same thing last summer. I figure it's a piece of cake. They'll have us in the database and I'll be outta here in a jiffy. Unfortunately, that is not at all how it plays out.

The registrar is a youngish woman with *enormous* bubble-shaped

101

bosoms and a very low-cut blouse that reveals a terrifying expanse of apparently bottomless cleavage. It is the day before July 4th vacation and she does not appear to be in such a terrific mood.

Nevertheless, I give her an attempted dazzling smile and explain that I'd like to re-register our little fishing boat before the holiday. With absolutely no affect, she taps the keyboard with 3-inch long plastic nails and then squinches her brow.

"We don't have anything under your husband's name with that date of birth owning a boat."

I take a deep breath. "That's interesting. I registered the boat right here at this very desk a year ago. It is a 1981 12 foot long aluminum Grumman with a 4.5 HP Evinrude outboard motor."

"Nope. Nothing." She starts to turn away to wait on the next customer.

"Wait. Wait…this is not working for me. You have to have this registration. I paid you $40.00 last summer."

She taps the keyboard harder, this time with emphasis to make her point. She sighs and flips her hair. I re-spell Tom's last name again L.A.J.O.I.E. and say his birth date very slowly as though, maybe, she is hearing impaired.

"I'm telling you we don't have anything with that name in the computer with a boat."

I pinch the bridge of my nose to try to prevent the gathering migraine.

She moves on to the next customer in line, bouncing her bodacious, unnaturally enhanced twin appendages.

I go back out to my car and call Tom on his cell. He is getting lobsters from our friend Perry Long on Newbury Neck. Tom says to just register the boat as if it is a new boat and forget it was ever registered before if it is so problematic. Okey-dokey, sure. Fab idea.

I go back in and stand in line. When it is my turn she says, "Weren't you just here?"

"Yes, but I'd like to register a new boat."

"OK, but you have to have a bill of sale."

Obviously, I don't have a bill of sale because *we've already registered the freakin' boat.* I slam my purse down on the counter. I'm about to have a stellar conniption fit, but instead, with admirable self-control, I regain my composure.

I plead shamelessly, "OK, look. I'm sure we can resolve this like adults. You've got to have the information…and I've got to register my boat. I'm trying to do the honest thing here and I'm trying to *give you my money.*"

She makes a huge sound of exasperation and says, threateningly, "Well, you're just going to have to talk to Bill in Augusta."

"OK, terrific, let's get Bill on the line." Bring him on. I'm feeling semi-encouraged.

She picks up a phone as though she can't believe this is really happening and speaks into the mouthpiece with clipped words, "Bill, there is a lady here who is *very persistent.* She won't leave until she can register her boat." To emphasize her point, she does a dramatic eye roll for the people behind me in line. She hands the phone to me.

I greet Bill thankfully and give him the same information. I wait for about two lifetimes while he checks the state database and he finally drawls back.

"No, dean, the only thing we got under Tom Lajoie with that birth date is a U-Haul."

"We don't own a U-Haul."

"Well, sure you do, deah. It was registered last yeah."

I'm beginning to feel like I am stuck in a perverse "Bert & I" skit… like "You Can't Get There From Heah"…only this is "You Don't Really Own A Boat…You Own A U-Haul."

"I don't know what to tell you. **We *don't own a U-Haul.***"

"Yuh. That's all we got. Anything else I can help you with, deah?"

I make a sound like a strangling cat. I can feel my blood pressure throbbing. Actually, I'm pretty sure I'm about to get a nosebleed.

"Listen, Bill, before you hang up. Can you read to me the description of our U-Haul?"

"Sho-ah. It's a 1981 12 foot long aluminum Grumman U-Haul."

"Let me guess, this U-Haul has a 4.5 Evinrude outboard motor?"

"Ayuh! How did you know, deah?"

Jaysus H. Christ.

The boobalicious registrar registers my U-Haul/boat but she's clearly annoyed that I have caused so many problems for her and her patient customers.

The next day, I'm talking this over with Tom, trying to come to grips with what happened.

Tom turns to me, his eyes wide, and he says, "Do you suppose it could possibly be because we originally told them our boat was a **V-Hull**?"

Yes. Yes, I do suppose…deah.

Tom and Carol in their U-Haul

How to Get Rid of
Unwanted Solicitors

For many years, I had members of a heretofore-unnamed religious group plaguing me by knocking on my door every couple of weeks. While I appreciated their fervor in wanting to save my soul from eternal damnation—and I agree, I probably require more assistance in that department than most—I feel that I am the captain of my own soul, so to speak, and I have the responsibility to find my own way to a safe shore or go down with the sinking ship.

Also, I belong to the Unitarian Universalist Church. While most churches have a cross over the entrance, the Unitarian church has a big question mark. We don't tend to get rabid about the superiority of one doctrine or denomination over another. I don't presume to speak for all Unitarians, but I'm pretty sure one of the core beliefs is that God isn't going to bail on whole groups of people because they don't have all the right answers—directly from the horse's mouth. Besides, *my* God is made in my image—in that She has breasts and a vagina.

Because of my refusal to be saved by them, I swear I became a training ground for new recruits. There they would be when I opened the door, all fresh-faced with rapturous zeal. I would mutter, "Oh, for chrissake" and they would beam in agreement. Let me explain: At my New Hampshire residence, I have a very long driveway that leads to a secluded property in the country with a sign that says "Private Drive." It actually takes some effort to find me; and because of this seclusion, I like to putter around outside in varying degrees of dress or undress.

The crowning invasion of my privacy came one day when I heard a muffled, "Help" coming from the other side of my front door. I heard it again, a little more insistent this time- "Help!" I swung the door open, and there was one of the proselytizers standing stone still with my dog Florence's teeth firmly embedded in his wrist. Every time he tried to move, Flo would growl ferociously and sink her teeth in a little firmer. I wanted to grin and say, "Good dog!" but instead, I said politely, "I already have a vacuum cleaner, thank you" and I closed the door.

After this episode, I visited our local police to see what I could do to stem the tide of saviors. They said if I had a sign that said "No Soliciting," then it would be illegal for anyone to come down my drive for that purpose. So that's what I did. I made a sign that said:

"NO SOLICTING—AND THIS MEANS *YOU!*"

I put it at the end of my driveway. It seemed to work like a charm for quite some time.

One day, on a blistering hot, muggy summer afternoon, I was nailing up some wooden lattice on my grape arbor in the back yard. On this particular day I had on a fabulous outfit—which consisted of *nothing* except a beautiful swath of antique, hand-beaded needlework that I got at a Native American auction in Los Angeles. The exquisite beadwork was on very soft doeskin that I assume was meant to be a bib front for a ceremonial dress or shirt. It was a beautiful piece and I tied it around my waist and wore it like a loincloth. There wasn't enough material to cover my butt, but that was okay, I thought it looked stunning. (Please do not panic – this was quite a few years ago. Now, in my sixties, I would never attempt this look. It would be way too terrifying.)

I was sweating bullets. It must've been 102 degrees. Rivulets of sweat and dirt were running down my torso. The dirt caked under my breasts and in the creases and rolls of my fat. I was covered with a sticky film of grime and perspiration. My face was streaked with mud.

That's when I heard Flo give a warning bark. I turned to see some people getting out of a car in my driveway. The women had on dainty lace collars. My mouth dropped open. I couldn't believe it. It got many degrees hotter as my blood began to boil.

My friend Kudra was working in the vegetable garden. To this day, she still talks about seeing this barbaric, prehistoric being—a dirty blur of slick skin and fringe and bright colored beads streaking across the back yard—an apparition that was slowly raising a hammer as it ran. I knew my bare breasts were swaying crazily from side to side as I ran, but I didn't care. By the time I got to the car, the hammer was high above my head. I was shaking with a white-hot rage.

I roared, ***"Tell me you're not soliciting!"***

The group looked horrified. They dove en masse into the car, screeched into reverse, and peeled out down the road in a cloud of dust.

It's been years now. I haven't seen anyone since. I highly recommend this technique—kind of a knockers for knockers approach—to rid yourself of unwanted evangelical visitors.

THONG LYME DISEASE

I had Lyme disease for several years in the early to mid-1990s. This was about a decade before it was identified as an epidemic in New Hampshire, so I was misdiagnosed every step of the way.

I know exactly how and where I got it. I was showing off for a lover. I was brushing back the edges of my back field with a weed whacker. The back field had this lovely small herd of deer that came out of the woods to graze at twilight every evening. I was wearing knee high rubber boots and safety glasses and a thong bathing suit. That was a fashion statement right there, I'll tell you what. Apparently, this look didn't impress my lover much, because the lover soon went back to California, never to be seen again. What I did get from that stellar outfit, however, was sick as a dog for years.

Not long after the bare-assed weed whacking, I noticed a small tick embedded in my upper thigh. I pulled it out, and it made a distinct "popping" sound when it released. I didn't think much about it—it was about this size: o. I do remember thinking that we didn't see ticks much at all when we were kids. Now ticks were becoming a pretty common occurrence, especially on our dogs.

In due time, I noticed a large crusty, angry red ring around the tick site—about the size of a saucer. I had read in some medical journals about a newly identified tick borne disease, named Lyme, after the town in Connecticut where it was first identified. The disease had also been found on Cape Cod in Massachusetts. I was positive that this was what was going on with my thigh, so I went to my family doctor. He took one look at my angry red saucer and said, "No, that's nothing."

Seriously?

He took a blood sample anyway to test for Lyme antibodies. The test came back negative. He sent me on my way.

(Years later, I asked this doctor why he ignored such a clear symptom as the obvious erythema migrans rash. He said, "Because Lyme wasn't in New Hampshire yet." I said, "What?!? You think these ticks know when they've crossed the state line? Don't you know that our highway signs say, '*Welcome to New Hampshire*'?")

I swear I felt it when the spirochetes began to spread throughout my body. I felt a rush of adrenaline and my heart began pounding. My whole body was on hyper-alert, as if sirens and alarms were screaming, *"DANGER! DANGER! DANGER!"* I remember thinking, "Aliens have just invaded my body."

Before long, I developed searing arthritis in both of my index fingers. I had a mean, headstrong horse at the time, so I thought maybe I had damaged my fingers by trying to rein her in. Honestly, the excuses I made for that damn disease were unbelievable. But the excuses didn't last long. The arthritis traveled quickly to all my joints until I was pretty debilitated with pain.

It was about this time that Tom and I hooked up. Right smack dab in the middle of it when I was a raving, crippled lunatic. Tom probably just thought this was normal behavior for me. I was so lucky that he loved me unconditionally. I guess it was good to have set the bar so low—it could only go up from there.

I tried everything. I prayed. I cried. I meditated. I visualized a healthy, pain free body. I did massage, Reiki, acupuncture. I hemorrhaged money. I saw healers and shamans and charlatans. Most of the charlatans wore white coats, by the way. Physicians told me I had all of the "hysterical woman" garbage can ailments. I was diagnosed with Chronic Fatigue Syndrome, Fibromyalgia, Epstein Barr Virus. One MD recommended that I take ibuprofen. I looked at him, "Are you serious? I'm eating ibuprofen like candy. If I had known, I would have invested in ibuprofen stock. I call it Vitamin I."

This is how crazy that disease was: One time I was on the train from New York City to Boston after meeting with my editor at Viking Penguin, sitting quietly with my eyes closed. I gasped as, out of the blue, I felt a screaming, scorching pain in my knee that lasted for about five minutes. Then I felt as though my shoulders were on fire, as if I'd been tasered. Then my jaw hurt so much that I couldn't bear it. Then my ankle felt as if it had been zapped with an electric cattle prod. Then a pain started deep down in my pelvis, like the pain of childbirth. *Holy Mother of God.* The pain traveled to five different joints in under thirty minutes. No wonder physicians thought I was nuts—this disease was freaking *INSANE!*

After the episode on the train, I said "F-this." I prescribed a 10-day course of antibiotics for myself. The antibiotics worked for several months. I had a short respite where I was deliriously pain free. Of course, we didn't know back then that wasn't long enough for an established disease like mine—and the aliens came back with a vengeance. They had multiplied exponentially.

I had good days and bad days. On a "good" day, I only felt dizzy and a little off –"a half bubble off plumb" as Tom called it. On bad days, I felt like I could end up in a wheelchair.

In the fourth summer, Tom and I traveled to British Columbia so Tom could kayak the melting glaciers with some of his extreme white water paddling friends. This is when I got *really* sick. I was running shuttle for the boaters, and I would go fly fishing while they ran the rapids – which was not easy, since I couldn't keep my arms up for more than five minutes without a break; I didn't have the strength. I would drive around those mountainous roads with one hand on the steering wheel while I rested the other hand in my lap. I couldn't raise my arms high enough to wash my hair. I tried doing strength training by flexing 15 oz. soup cans.

Finally, the arthritis moved into my jaw so I couldn't eat. I got a Bell's palsy in the right side of my face, so it drooped a little bit. Then it moved into my ear. My ear was scorching hot to the touch, turned red and swelled up to the size of an apple. I think the stress of the spirochetes triggered a herpes zoster-"shingles"-infection in my face. I was a mess. I think I tried another course of antibiotics somewhere in here, but it didn't touch it.

I was a mess...but I was in love. Tom and I slept in the back of our Jeep with the dogs. We were amidst the most beautiful landscapes I had ever witnessed. Rolling thunder and lightning spiraling in a glacial bowl. The Houndstooth Glacier in Bugaboo Park. Lake Louise. (And on the downside, the horrific mosquitoes in McBride, British Columbia.)

It was in Whistler, when I couldn't walk any longer and had to sit down on the sidewalk, that we decided to go home.

Somewhere east of the Rockies, I said to Tom, "I don't want to jinx myself...but I think it's gone."

Tom was driving, so he was looking straight ahead. "What's gone?"

"'IT' ...the aliens. I think the aliens have packed up and moved out."

And it was true. Miraculously, I was fine. No pain, no arthritis. Just gone, as if it had never happened. Days later, when we got home, I said to Tom, "Look!" and I did a cartwheel.

Moral of the story: Never *ever* show off by wearing only a thong when working in the woods in New England.

Postscript: I am, understandably, completely freaked out about the possibility of being infected with Lyme again. That is why I travel with Doxycycline at all times. The CDC's current recommendation is to take as prophylaxis a single dose of Doxy (200 mg) after exposure to a deer tick bite. I double this. I don't care if it makes me nauseous. I have done this protocol a few times over the past decade and I believe it has served me well.

I do not know why my infection left my body when and how it did. There is really no explanation. I hadn't done anything special. I realize that this is not a normal scenario and that the outcome is usually a lot more dire. All I know is that I have been symptom-free ever since. I believe I may have been "herxing" when I was so sick in Whistler that I couldn't stand up. The worsening of my symptoms at that moment may have been a result of a die-off of the bacteria in my system. I don't know.

What I do know is this: I had been a widow for many years, and now I was going home with the man who was to become my husband. That's it.

COBB

Many years ago now, when I was still a sprightly middle-aged young thing, I was driving home from an appointment in Antrim when I saw an ancient old man on the side of the road with his thumb stuck out. As I sped by him, I thought, "Holy mackerel, that man has got to be 100 years old!" Of course, I turned around to pick him up. The man struggled to get in my car, so I went around to the passenger side to give his brittle bones a gentle hoist up.

The man grinned a toothless grin and said, "The name's Cobb."

I said, "Well, hello there, Cobb. Where to?"

He said he was heading to the American Legion Hall in Hillsboro for the day. He perched happily on the passenger seat and started talking non-stop. He told me that he was 97 years old and worked all his life on the B&M (Boston & Maine) railroad in Hillsboro before it closed down. He was proud that he had been a brakeman for the Hillsboro line, and he regaled me for the 15-minute drive with stories of what it was like to work on the railroad in its heyday in the beginning of the 20th century. A very educational monologue, I must say.

When we got to the Legion hall, Cobb again struggled to get out of my car, so I went around to the passenger side to give him a hand. When his feet hit the ground and he stood up, his pants fell down. Fell. Right down to the ground. He had on some ratty old boxer shorts underneath.

Cobb looked at me with his rheumy eyes and said, "Aw, my damn belt is too big."

I knelt down in front of him and pulled up his pants and tried to cinch his belt tighter around his tiny waist to prevent him from further embarrassment. As I was fumbling with his belt, I happened to look up into the front window of the Legion hall. There were about twenty men with their faces practically smashed against the glass. Have you ever seen those cartoon faces where the eyeballs pop out on springs? That'd be them…every single one.

When Cobb finally walked through the front door, I heard hooting and catcalls and whistles. One drunk voice hollered out, "Holy shit, Cobb! That was friggin' awesome!"

FALL

MURMURATION

I just heard and saw (mostly *heard*) the most amazing thing—about 10,000 black birds just congregated in the trees along our field. They were making the most incredible *NOISE!* It sounded like thousands of monkeys screeching or hundreds of really rusty, grinding, shorting-out machines. Mostly, the birds sounded really *excited!* Excited to be on their journey, excited to be retracing the precise path to South America that their ancestors took millions of years before them.

Just before they departed, the noise escalated to a roar that sounded like a jet plane landing in the field. My mouth dropped open. I grinned. It sounded exactly like the roar in a Dead show just as everyone peaks together. Magic. Then they flew off in a huge black double-helix cloud. (I later found out that this "double-helix" phenomenon of a black bird migration is called a Murmuration.)

Adios and Godspeed black birds—may you arrive safely in the land of your ancestors.

ANTLIONS AND INVADERS FROM MARS

When I was about eleven years old, in the very early 1960s, I watched a movie by myself called *Invaders from Mars*. I was sitting downstairs in our dark basement "rec room" and I got terrified beyond all rationality. In the movie, a young boy about my age sees a spaceship slip under the sand in a sand pit next to his house. People who walked across that area were sucked down under the sand into tunnels to the spaceship. There the Martians drilled holes in the nape of their necks and inserted mind-control electrodes into their brain stems.

I remember I was eating walnuts as I watched the movie. I was nervously cracking whole walnuts and picking out the meat and frantically munching them as I watched, spellbound and horrified. I ate a *lot* of walnuts. About the time the head Martian appears in the movie—and he was literally only a *HEAD*—I started to get a bitter aftertaste of stale walnuts in the back of my throat. I ran to the closet bathroom just in time to throw up.

At the time, I had a little cowpony named Liberty Belle. My father and I had built a small stable for my horse in a field next to our house—a field that was on the far side of our septic tank's leach field. Unfortunately, the leach field was large, and was all sand. There was no way in hell I was going

120

to walk across that leach field and get sucked under the sand. I had to carry two water buckets to Belle every morning and every night. I walked with those heavy buckets all the way *around* the leach field for many years. By the time I was in my late teens, I was extremely proud of how muscular my arms were. I could win a bicep contest with a boy any day.

Predictably, that movie scarred me for being able to watch any sci-fi horror movies ever again. I did try two more times. When I was a freshman in high school, I tried to watch *Psycho* in a movie theater with a bunch of friends. About the time they find the "mother" in the cellar, I had to run to the ladies room. My friends gave me grief about that for a long time. The last movie I attempted was *Alien*. I was an adult, and I thought surely I'd out grown my ridiculous freak-outs with all things extraterrestrial. Besides, someone said it was "funny" and not scary at all. Right. Same result—but this time I blamed throwing up on too much wine.

Flash forward to the present: After I strapped my two lovely new EpiPens around my waist, Tom and I went walking in the woods. We ambled along aimlessly until we came to an old sand pit. Tom grinned hugely and crouched down, and pointed to a small indentation in the sand. It was only about the size of a quarter. I never would have noticed it as anything special if he hadn't pointed it out. He said it was the lair of an antlion, and that when he was a kid, he and his brothers used to torture ants for hours in a sand pit near their home.

With this non-explanation, Tom got up and rolled over a rotten log, and grabbed a hapless ant. He dropped the ant down in the center of the sand saucer. All of a sudden, two huge pincer jaws exploded out of the sand and grabbed the ant! There was sand flying everywhere as the ant struggled desperately; but then it disappeared under the surface. Gone. All was quiet.

My mouth was dropped open. *Holy Martian Reprise!* Tom was grinning at me. Immediately, I got a bitter aftertaste of stale walnuts in the back of my throat. I knew what was going to happen next.

I ran to the bushes.

MY VAGINA GETS ME OUT OF A SPEEDING TICKET

About a year after almost dying from anaphylactic shock from a random yellow jacket sting, I was hiking in the late summer on a trail in the Hopkinton Greenway with my neighbor and our dogs. We were ambling along with our mutts when she yelled that something was in her hair. I went to swat it out, when I saw it was a yellow jacket angrily buzzing in her dark tresses. I jumped back saying, "Oh, shit, this could be really bad."

It was then that I felt a sharp sting in my ankle…then another in my side…then another on my neck.

"Holy Crap! We're standing on a ground nest of yellow jackets!" I bellowed.

Expecting at any moment to see scenes from my life flash before my eyes, I wailed, "This could kill me!" and I lit off back toward the beginning of the trail—which also happened to be right behind the Hopkinton Police Department.

In my defense, I did have a fanny pack (which I have lately been told by a daughter of a friend that this is pathetically uncool and unhip in an old-lady kind of way) in which I carried two EpiPens, some Benadryl capsules and a small envelope of homeopathic Apis Mellifica (bee venom). I poured the Apis under my tongue as I ran, waited a few minutes for it to dissolve, then started crunching Benadryl as I sprinted. I think I ingested at least six Benadryls by the time I made it back to the police station. I was waiting to inject myself with the epinephrine until if/when I started to exhibit signs of shock.

I was pretty freaked out by the time I made it the police station. I told them my history, and they looked pretty worried too. I said that the last time was so severe; that I had been told the next time would surely be lethal. They called an ambulance, and the paramedics arrived within mere minutes. I told the paramedics about needing to be intubated the last time I was stung, so they were hovering around like flies, hoping they'd get to practice on me. We sat...they took my vitals...we sat some more. I was waiting to get sweaty and faint and anoxic. Nothing appeared to be happening.

Finally, the Chief of Police asked if I felt like I was going into shock, if I felt like I was having any kind of reaction.

I thought for a moment, and then said honestly, "No, actually, the last time the first thing that happened was that my vagina was on *fire*. My vagina swelled up crazily from an allergic reaction to the toxin. I credit this with saving my life—for which I am eternally grateful. But right now I feel fine."

To his credit, the Police Chief only coughed a little...politely. We waited a bit more, but when nothing dramatic occurred, my friend drove me home. I had a glass of wine, and with that—combined with the six Benadryls I had inhaled on my run and the immense relief of knowing that being stung wasn't an automatic death sentence —I slept until the next day.

A couple of weeks later, I was driving down my road to the grocery store when I got pulled over by a young Hopkinton cop for speeding. I always forget that the speed limit drops stupidly, randomly about a mile from my house. It was a cop that I didn't recognize; he must've been a newby. He asked if I was speeding to go to a delivery (my plates say MIDWYF). I said no, I was just going to the store for wine. He took my license and went back to his cruiser.

Several minutes later, he returned and handed me back my license. He couldn't make eye contact, his face was very red and he looked like he was about to choke with laughter. He said, "You're good. You're all set. Have a good day." He was still looking at the ground.

As I drove away, it dawned on me what had happened. I knew damn well that when he radioed into the station, they said, "That's *HER*! That's the one with the swollen vagina!"

I grinned. Well, HOT SHIT! My vagina saves me yet again.

Sumbitchin Barn
Building Details

Tom's barn at Bad Beaver

Tom had been building his barn in his head for several years before the actual work commenced. He would get a glazed-over, distant look in his eyes and I just knew he was calculating how many trees he was going to have to saw into lumber to make it all work. It was either that…or he was having an affair.

But because he had the barn plans festering in that incredible brain of his for so long, by the time he started physically building it, the 30' x 70', 4200 sq. ft. barn was structurally completed and weather-tight in only 13 days. And seriously, with all that thinking and planning, not to mention the execution, the poor guy doesn't have the time or energy to pick up his socks, never mind have an affair.

The first part of the barn to arrive at Bad Beaver was half a dozen *enormous* steel I-beams that were salvaged from a NH highway overpass. Tom's friend, Peter Webster, who owns Cohen Steel in Concord, was cleaning out his steel yard and wanted to get rid of them. When Tom agreed to take them, he had no idea what he was going to use them for. It was just a matter of, how could you refuse a gift of I-beams, even if they did weigh 4000 pounds apiece? You never know when you might need an emergency I-beam.

The shortest of the beams was 30 feet long. These were unceremoniously dumped from the tractor-trailer that transported them, at the end of our drive out at the Red Bridge Road. Tom carried them down our road with his old 1972 400B LULL all-terrain forklift. The weight of each beam was the maximum carrying capacity of the old girl, but she did it. Of course, our drive wasn't 30 feet wide, so Tom had to cut down a bunch of trees along the way to get the beams down the road to our field. And there they stayed for several years, marinating, right next to the lovely old ranch gate at the entrance to our field—right where I had to see them stacked in a formidable mountain of hulking steel every time I went out into the world. It was the most redneck-looking thing imaginable. It made me grumpy and gave me something to bitch about for four years. And believe me, bitch I did.

It was when Tom decided that he would use the I-beams to support the second floor of his barn, so he wouldn't have any structural columns in the way, so he could drive his equipment around on the first floor of the barn, that I secretly stopped bitching. I could see the method in his madness.

(This is what usually happens to my bitching, Tom finds some maniacal, miraculous use for all the crap that he hauls home, and I have to acquiesce.)

Then Tom got that dreamy, faraway look again, figured out how much weight steel support columns on the exterior walls would have to bear—and engineered the plans for the bump-outs in the foundation to support these pilasters. (I know…I get exhausted just *writing* about how his brain works.)

He called his friend Peter Webster again and told him what he needed to hold up the I-beams. Peter said he just happened to have some steel 8" x 8" columns down in the "dog leg" of his yard. (I don't know what that means either; this is what Tom said when I was interviewing him for this story.) Peter cut them to length and trucked them up to Ellsworth. Tom cut the I-beams all to 30 feet with an acetylene torch and then drilled holes in the steel with a Mag Drill so the beams and the support columns could be bolted together. Tom had it so precisely engineered ahead of construction, that when the time came to raise the beams the whole thing went up like a giant erector set.

Ken Thompson poured the foundation for the barn. Tom designed it, and Kenny built the frames for the cement and poured it according to Tom's directions. They did a very professional job, albeit with Tom fussing and "supervising" the entire time. Well, this *was* his baby, after all. The area around the barn was expanded and graveled with material from our own gravel pit. It was starting to look like a Wal-Mart parking lot. Then the foundation sat for two years.

We were still coming up from New Hampshire every other weekend. It was insane. Ten hours of driving for one full day of working our asses off. Our house in NH was on the market, but it was the worst time in human history to try to sell real estate. In the interim, Tom and his brother, Lee, and his dad, Leo, were cutting our trees into lumber for the barn with Tom's Wood-Mizer sawmill. Tom would place a tree on the sawmill with his LULL and they would cut it into boards that were then stickered in huge piles in lumberyards on our land to dry. Tom had an extension for his mill so they could cut the roof rafters for the barn that were 26' foot long 2" x 10"s. There were huge orderly stacks of wood drying everywhere.

Then in late September of 2011, the stars—and other circumstances—aligned properly for us to be able to begin construction on the Bad Beaver barn. We were all pretty excited to get building after waiting for two years. Tom's left-hand man, his most trusted and skilled helper, Liam "Casey" O'Brien came up to stay with us for two weeks to "git 'er done." It just felt good to be finally moving forward and I knew Tom was going to push it to the limit.

I was doing my best demure Snow White imitation, staying at Camp Kwitchabitchin and cooking and cleaning for a crew of sometimes up to five men and four dogs. I would see the guys off to work on the barn every morning with their tool belts and nail guns, except my dwarfs were named Stinky, Overachiever, Dysfunctional, Pukey and Grumpy. *Hi HO!*

Tom was so focused he became almost silent—well, during the day, anyway. At night there was a significant amount of beer consumed by all and lots of redneckedness. But they deserved it, everyone worked like hell. Tom trucked up his second LULL, his "new" 1995 844B, to be able to handle the raising of the 4000-pound I-beams. The two LULLs did an intricate dance with each other as they lifted each I-beam into place. I have to admit, it made me a tad giddy to see these incredible machines holding the dangling behemoths overhead as Tom gently nudged them into their pre-drilled holes. I found I was holding my breath as if one exhale from me would send the whole thing crashing down.

At one point, I saw Tom sitting still in his LULL, silently stroking his goatee. I knew that pensive gesture. He was thinking, "Jesus, I hope this goes together like I think it will." In the end, all I-beams were safely in their cradles and the first floor was complete—and it was only day six! I have a great photo of Tom, Casey, Leo and Lee sitting on top of the last I-beam. It reminds me of that iconic picture of the steelworkers eating their lunch on a skyscraper in Manhattan, except the Bad Beaver workers were celebrating by drinking a beer.

Tom sheathed the exterior of the first floor by using a chevron pattern with the boards, as he says this makes it stronger and less likely to move. He framed the upstairs floor with 4 foot flipped floor joists along the sides to prevent ballooning of the knee-wall upstairs and to stop the downstairs from blowing out. It is 16' 9" from foundation to the top plate.

On the ninth day, there was a torrential downpour. It was a totally shitty, miserable, soaking day. Tom and Casey hung around the camp drying their clothes by the wood stove, playing cards and complaining bitterly about losing a day.

Tom and Casey getting ready for the roof rafters

When the weather finally cleared, Tom and Casey were back on the job bright and early. They built the gable ends lying on the second floor deck, then raised them by standing them up with the LULL. Tom said the most potentially disastrous event occurred with the raising of the SW gable. He was running the LULL, and Casey was inside upstairs holding on to a rope attached to the overhang. After standing the gable up, Tom went to check on Casey. Casey was holding on for dear life, his feet braced fiercely against the deck.

Casey yelled, "I think she's a half-bubble off plum!"

Actually, the gable was 15 to 20 degrees beyond plum, leaning precipitously two stories above the ground. Tom ran back down to the LULL and pushed the gable back in.

Tom said of that situation: "The only thing that prevented the whole thing from crashing to the ground was Casey holding on to that rope. He was holding on like he was belaying his best friend on Mount Everest."

I don't know where I was at the time, but I'm glad I didn't see that. I don't think all the screaming would've been helpful at all.

We had many visitors stop by to help or just gawk. Lots of family and friends wandered in and out to participate when they could. Even Tom's mother, Caryl Lajoie, got sucked into running the chop-saw, cutting the 30-inch cedar gable overhangs. She said she loved it.

I think the most impressive part (well, after you get over the insane mania of the steel I-beams), the most *visually* impressive part of the whole thing, is the roof rafters. I love the way they look. They are so overwhelming that when people go upstairs, they just stop in their tracks and do a low whistle. You just can't help it. It's like being in the belly of the whale.

Tom and Casey organized all the roof rafters the day before they planned to raise them. There were 120 rafters lined up and ready to go. Each rafter was 26 feet long and weighed 150 lbs. The boys started precisely at 7:00 AM. Casey was up on a catwalk staging at the peak, waiting for Tom to hoist a rafter up to him to nail in place. Tom lifted every single one of those rafters, with his own sweet little body, up to Casey in ONE DAY. I was on the second floor photographing this and it made me almost weep with how hard Tom worked that day, the exertion that that boy mustered up to get those rafters in place. I was fearful that his heart might burst—or at the very least, that he might get a massive hernia.

That night I think the boys had ibuprofen for dinner. By the time I got food on the table, they were both sound asleep.

Just when we thought we had conquered the beast, another much larger monster reared its formidable head. The roof had to be plywooded and they had only one day left to do it. It was now Day 13, and the next day we were packing it all up to go back home to New Hampshire. The barn has a 26-foot roof that is a 12 pitch. That meant that there were 120 sheets of plywood needed to sheath the entire roof. Tom and Casey carried each sheet of plywood up that steep pitch and slammed them down and nailed them in place.

As Tom so succinctly described it, "It sucked."

Now Tom was pushing mercilessly. Pushing himself and pushing poor Casey beyond the limits of what the human body can endure. Casey is such a Zen calm, even-keeled guy. If it had been me, I would have demanded a divorce. I would have called the Labor Department, and then the Department of Employment Security, and Tom would be looking for his second wife.

But Tom and Casey got it weather-tight by nightfall. They covered the entire roof with Roof Top Guard #2, which is a waterproof synthetic paper. They stapled it all in place with a plastic-tab gun. In short, they worked their adorable butts off.

When I congratulated Tom for pulling it off, he just grinned. "This is what we do every day," he said. "Brute force and ignorance. You just put your head down and do it."

But I know he was damn proud of what they had accomplished. The photo at the beginning of this story is one I took as Tom and Casey posed proudly with their work of art at nightfall on the 13th day. They had done it, and lived to tell the tale. They had created a breathtaking structure and they had beaten the clock. I was pretty damn proud of them too.

The roof rafters upstairs in the new barn. There are 150 rafters–all cut from our own trees!

THE BUILDING OF TOM'S BARN
A 14-DAY PICTORIAL OF BUILDING
THE BARN AT
BAD BEAVER

BUILDING SUMBITCHIN BARN ~ WEEK ONE

DAY ONE ~ Two cute guys, Tom Lajoie & Liam (Casey) O'Brien, start the day with all the dogs.

DAY TWO - Tom's maniacal engineering. The second floor is supported with 4 enormous (30') steel I beams from a NH highway overpass. The whole thing went up like a giant erector set with the help of his two LULLS. Now Tom can drive all his equipment around inside the barn without being hampered by columns (a must have, apparently, in a man-cave-barn).

DAY THREE - Camp Kwitchabitchin. This is the little camp Tom built for me so I could play Snow White, cooking and cleaning for the crew (and paint all the frickin windows for the barn).

DAY FOUR ~ The barn raisers enjoying a beverage at the end of a hard day: Tom Lajoie, Liam O'Brien, Leo Lajoie, Lee Lajoie

DAY FIVE ~ The fifth and final bay going up. Tom cut all the lumber used for the barn from our own trees with his sawmill!

DAY SIX ~ The first floor is up…now on to the second floor and the big observation cupola.

DAY SEVEN ~ The intrepid crew at Bad Beaver…thank you Leo, Lee, Liam, Tom (& Phaedra, Gladys, Bailey, Matilda.) Now on to bean-hole beans and beer!

BUILDING SUMBITCHIN BARN ~ WEEK TWO

DAY EIGHT ~ My hottie husband, Tom Lajoie, putting down the second floor deck (with Matilda sniffing his man bits).

DAY NINE - Back at the camp…totally shitty, miserable, soaked day. The guys got rained out by a torrential downpour. Tom and Liam hung around the camp drying their clothes by the wood stove, playing cribbage and complaining bitterly about losing a day.

DAY TEN ~ There are 120 roof rafters in the barn. Tom cut all the lumber for the barn *from our own trees with his sawmill!* The roof rafters are HUGE. They are 2 x 10 x 30' and weigh 150 lbs. each. Tom physically lifted every single one up to Liam who was waiting up on a catwalk. They got all 120 rafters in place in one day. Lots of ibuprophen for dinner that night.

In the Belly of the Whale

DAY ELEVEN ~ This is my favorite photo of building the barn—with all of Tom's roof rafters in place and the roof going on. I call it "In the Belly of the Whale."

DAY TWELVE ~ Tom and Liam pushing like hell to finish the final side of the roof and get it weather-tight by nightfall.

DAY THIRTEEN ~ They did it! They beat the clock! They built a 30' x 70', 4200 sq. ft. barn in under two weeks – and it is stunning. Here are Tom and Liam posing with their work of art at nightfall on the 13th day. The barn looks like an antique New England barn from the drive and the gable ends. The far side has 5 huge bays for all of Tom's equipment.

A great quote overheard from Tom describing his structure: "The first impression of the barn is one of New England tranquility. The far side looks like Jiffy Lube."

DAY FOURTEEN - Tom contemplating his feat. I am so proud of him…he rocked it! Designed and engineered by Tom Lajoie, phenomenal "economy of motion" builder.

THE FOLLOWING WEEKEND ~ Carol and Kendall Temper at a barn-warming party, where Carol is (probably) exclaiming about what an ingenious builder Tom is. Doesn't it look like Kendall is saying, "Please make her stop!"

The barn (the Jiffy Lube side) with the new doors ~ 2014

CHIEF WOUNDED PECKER

Tom is working with his left-hand man, Liam "Casey" O'Brien, in Orono building a spec-house for a Serbian entrepreneur/brew-master friend of ours. I have to stay home in NH as I am being trained to do OB ultrasounds at the health center. Tom and Casey have been staying at Bad Beaver and commuting to Orono every day. They've been up there for two weeks now.

Tom calls me late one afternoon and our conversation goes something like this:

T: "Hi honey!"
C: "Hey! How're you doing?"
T: "Oh, I'm OK."
C: "Just 'OK'? What are you doing?"
T: "I'm driving back from the doctor's office."
C: "*The doctor's office?!?* What do you mean 'the doctor's office'? You *never* go to the doctor. What happened?"
T: "Well, it's a little hard to explain. Actually, it's kind of embarrassing."
C: "Try me."
T: "Well, Casey and I were removing a post that was a support for a porch roof. It came down faster than I anticipated and it had a nail sticking out of the end of it. It came down with a helluva force…the nail ripped through the front of my pants and sliced my penis all the way down the shaft."

There is dead silence for a moment. I have no words. Who does this?!?

C: "Oh my god! Are you kidding? Are you going to be all right? How serious is it?"
T: "The doctor said he couldn't stitch it because the skin is too thin. So he just cleaned it up and put a bunch of butterfly bandages on it. He says it'll heal OK."

I start to smile. Actually, I am unsuccessfully trying to suppress a belly laugh.

C: "OK…let me get this straight. You just filleted your pecker?"
T: "Yeah, and I asked Casey to help me. He just said, 'You're going to die.'"
C: "How many butterflies died for this operation?"
T: "There are about 30 to cover the whole length."
C: "Ha. Ha. You know, it's probably a good thing that little chubby stepped up to the plate and took a hit for the team. If it had been to either side, it could've sliced your femoral artery—and you'd be dead."

Then a thought occurs to me.

C: "So, how long did the doctor say you had to keep your hands off it and leave it alone?"
T: "He said a week or so should do it."
C: "Right. Good luck with that, Mr. Whack Noodle."

Tom comes home for a break two days later. I look at his poor patched-up penis. It has several butterfly bandages along a long slice.
I can't help it. "Ewww…*Frankenschlong.*"
"Very funny."
But the very next morning, I swear to god, the boy wakes up and gives me the kooky eye.
I cannot believe it. He is delusional.
"I WILL NOT HAVE BUTTERFLIES IN MY VAGINA!"
Then a week later, he comes home and tries it again. By now the slice has healed into a curve—which looks disturbingly like a Smiley Face.
He says, "Look! He's happy to see you!"

GUTTER WOMEN

Carol doing CPR on a male black bear

Carol Leonard

Déjà vu. It is the first day of school. Only this time I am riding in a long yellow school bus full of excited, screeching women who are headed to the shooting range. The "shooters" all have on pink Ruger caps given to them by the gun company. They bounce along down the road in their matching caps, happy campers leaning over seatbacks to be heard better, yelling and switching seats like fifth graders. The energy is high and there are a lot of them. This is the first time shooting for many of them.

I, on the other hand, am in the way back with my eight other classmates. We are like the bad girls who used to sneak cigarettes in the back seat of the bus. We are the "gutters" and I do believe that the rest of the women on the bus may be avoiding us—the crazy women who are about to disembowel some large cute mammals.

I don't know anybody so I strike up a conversation with my seatmate—she is an attractive redhead with a big smile. It turns out she has lived in Moscow on and off for the past fifteen years. I worked as a midwife in the "radoms," or maternity hospitals, in Moscow in the early 1990s, so we have a great conversation about the deplorable state of women's healthcare in Russia. We chat with occasional Ruskie phrases sprinkled in our language. She had much the same experience I did with the realization that Russia is really an impoverished third-world country. I like her immediately.

The shooters are dropped off at the firing range and the nine of us continue on to our "Field Dressing Big Game" class. We come to a clearing in the woods and the sight is initially very shocking. There are eight deer carcasses and one bloated black bear lying on the ground, roughly in a circle. It looks like the aftermath of a horrible attack. Carnage everywhere.

The deer all have broken legs; these animals are road kills. NH Fish and Game has gathered these animals and kept them in a freezer waiting specifically for this class. The first thing that assails me is the horrific *smell*. Our instructors tell us to shove Vicks VapoRub up our nostrils to disguise the odor. This works—temporarily. I have to renew my gooey nose plug several times over the course of the next few hours.

Our main instructor is a burly retired Fish and Game warden named John. He is exactly as I imagined he would be; seasoned, knowledgeable and patient. He also has a dry sense of humor—a very necessary trait in this line of work. He starts the gutting of a large doe immediately after briefing us about knife safety and sharpening. One classmate is afraid she

150

might be sick, but after John's demonstration and straightforward anatomy lesson, all of my classmates are eager to dig in.

I pick a smallish doe because a Mourning Cloak butterfly has landed on her nose. Bambi. I am a little disconcerted by all the flies, but after I make the first incision and open her up, I relax and am in my element. This is all very familiar to me; skin, fascia, muscle. The hunting knife is extremely sharp and the eviscerating goes easily. I have a little bit of a struggle with the esophagus and I have to go in up to my elbows but soon the entire mass of entrails breaks free in a glistening pile and slides onto the ground. Out of curiosity, I open up the stomach and find my little doe had been eating beechnuts. Sweet thing. I feel confident that I can field dress game now to cool down the meat.

The last lonely carcass is that of a male black bear whose abdomen is expanded as tight as a drum. I think we have all been avoiding him because he is so bloated; he looks like he will explode in a burst of foul-smelling gas with the first incision. So, of course, John asks me to do the honors.

John says, "Carol, so now you have your game. You are all alone in the woods. Now what do you do?"

Something about the way he says this causes me to automatically drop to my knees at the bear's side and shout,

"Call 911!"

I shake the bear and say, "Bear! Bear! Are you alright?"

No response. I find the xyphoid process and position my hands and begin CPR (well, the C-part anyway—the pulmonary part would be virtually impossible because his teeth are sticking out about four inches from his lips).

John looks around warily and says, "Jaysus, you women are seriously starting to scare me."

And I was right. This bear is so unbelievably stanky that *no* amount of Vicks VapoRub is going to prevent this gag-fest. *Holy Ursus!* I smell this poor rotting bruin on my fingers for days. But I sincerely thank his Bear Spirit for allowing me to learn from him.

On the bus ride back to camp, I chat with another gutter in my class. It turns out she did all the black and white photographs in the original edition of *Our Bodies, Ourselves.* Wow! We have a poignant recollection about running around with speculums looking at cervices during the height of the Self-Help Movement of the 1970s. I am astounded.

Where else on earth could you possibly eviscerate an animal and then have a scholarly discussion about global women's health?

PHEASANT HUNTING
WITH OLD CROW

Carol dressing an upland bird

I have an old friend, Crow Dickinson, who was called the "Dean" of the NH House of Representatives, as he was the longest-standing legislator in the House with 32 years of consecutive terms. He was first elected in 1974 and served until his retirement in 2006. Crow was also instrumental in helping the NH midwives get our first ever in the country Board of Midwifery that is a state licensing agency that regulates the practice of midwifery. Crow was the New Hampshire midwives' staunchest champion.

Crow is a true Yankee blue blood, New Hampshire's version of aristocracy. Crow's real name is Howard but he is called Crow because, well, he actually looks like a crow. He is a huge man with white hair and a hooked beak, and he has the habit of tipping his head sideways with an intense beady-eyed expression when he thinks someone is bullshitting him. He looks exactly like a crow that has spied something shiny or is homing in on some road kill.

After his infamous stint in the legislature, Crow retired to his antique cape in the North Country and his 1000-acre kingdom on a mountaintop with majestic views of snow-capped Mount Washington in the background. Crow is also a life-long avid hunter and gun collector.

One day in late Fall, Crow asked me if I would like to go pheasant hunting with him. I said, "Sure!" I would love to have some game birds in my freezer.

Crow picked me up before dawn on a freezing cold day. I dressed in many layers of warm clothing that I'd scrounged and we set off in his funky old Bronco full of firearms. He gave me a tutorial about the etiquette of shooting in what he described as a "well-designed driven shoot." I had previously been given some pistol shooting lessons with a friend who was a pro at the local firing range, so I was fairly confident of my aim.

We drove several towns over to an exclusive "members only" sporting club that provided their own birds. When we got there, a couple dozen men and a few women were standing around a bar drinking coffee and talking about ammo. I felt a little out of place, so I wandered around looking at all the stuffed/taxidermy animal specimens that lined every wall. I was beginning to wonder if this was such a sane idea.

The "shoot" consisted of a very large, irregular circle with 12 shooting stations around the perimeter that had 2 guns (people) to each peg. Crow and I walked to our first shooting position and waited until an air-horn blasted loudly announcing that birds were being released from a platform in the center and it was time to load. By the time I was loaded, all the birds had soared over my head and were probably safely nesting and raising their young in Hillsboro by the time I was ready to shoot them. With the next air-horn blast, it was time to unload and walk to the next station.

I was shooting one of Crow's favorite guns, a Benelli 20 gauge automatic that shot 3-inch shells of #6 birdshot. It was a really nice looking sleek, sexy black shotgun. I was finally getting a little faster at loading and actually took a few pot shots at birds that flew frantically toward the perimeter of the circle as 24 people blasted away at them.

BLAM! BLAM! BLAM-BLAM!

I was trying to look up to see the birds as torrents of birdshot came raining down into my eyes and face. I felt like I would be eating gunpowder and grit for the next three weeks.

The "money bird," which was a gorgeous male pheasant with a strip of neon surveyor's tape tied to its leg, flew past us and Crow shot him in a heartbeat. This meant Crow got the prize of $250 for that special bird—which also meant now his expenses were even for sponsoring me. I was getting really excited.

At the next station, when the air-horn blasted, I quickly reached into my pocket to get a bunch of shells to re-load. My heart was pounding. Without looking, I dropped the shells in the chamber.

Just as I was about to raise the Benelli, Crow screamed at me.

"Whoa! Whoa! *WHOA!* What the hell was that?!?"

He grabbed my gun and unloaded it. He had been watching me out of the corner of his beady, avian eye. Out popped my Bonnie Bell Dr. Pepper Lip Smacker lip-gloss—which happened to be about the same size as a 3-inch shell—and which also happened to be in my coat pocket at the same time.

"Jesus Christ, Leonard, you're about to get us both killed."

"Sorry."

Moral of the story: Never put your lipstick in the same pocket as your ammo.

On the very last peg, a beautiful male ring-neck flew right in front of me at the perfect height. I squeezed the trigger and down he came. I couldn't believe it. I turned to Crow and grinned. This was the nuts!

At the end of the shoot, everyone re-convened at the bar for shots of whiskey and cigars. There were lots of inflated stories of skill and bravado, camaraderie and much guffawing and posturing.

When it came time to leave, I wanted to take my bird home to cook him. There was a pile of pheasants outside about four feet high. I was astounded. I asked Crow; didn't people take their birds home to eat them? He said some did…most didn't. The dog handlers took a few of the best birds. I was appalled. I picked through the pile to find the birds that were the most intact and with the least amount of birdshot in them. I found eight beautiful birds that I claimed for my own and brought them home with me.

When I got them home, I skinned them by using the old Yankee method of removing the whole pelt instead of plucking. Here's how you do it: Place the bird on its back and spread the wings out and step on the "armpits" of the bird. Place your toes right where the wing joins the body. Firmly grasp the legs and pull, and the whole pelt of feathers slides off easily, like removing your overcoat. This way you have a clean, skinless breast. Then you just have to cut off the wings and clean out the innards.

One time I cooked a Guinea fowl hen that I had raised. I decided to roast her, so I placed her in a pan with two strips of bacon crossed in an X over her breast. When I took her out of the oven she had shrunk down to the size of a canary. It reminded me of the scene in *What Ever Happened to Baby Jane* where Bette Davis served her sister, Anne Bancroft, her sister's pet parrot that she had roasted. "Eat your din-din."

This time I decided I would cook these birds by pan frying them and then simmering them to keep them as moist as possible. Here's the recipe I made up:

Wild Pheasant in Sour Cream

2 pheasants (about 3 lbs. each), quartered
Coarse cracked black pepper
Unbleached white flour
¼ C (or more as needed) extra virgin olive oil
4 smashed garlic cloves
1 can low sodium chicken broth
1 bottle of good Chardonnay (1 C for the birds and
the rest for drinking while cooking)
1 t dried rosemary
1 pint low fat sour cream

Rinse the pheasants, pat dry. Sprinkle lightly with pepper, then dredge in flour, shaking off excess. Heat about 3 T of the EVOO in a Dutch oven; add the pheasant, a few pieces at a time, and brown well on all sides. As pieces are browned, set them aside. Add more oil if needed. Drink a glass of wine.

When all the pheasant is browned, add the garlic to the pot and stir until golden, then blend in broth, wine, rosemary. Return the pheasants to the pot, bring juices to a boil, reduce heat, cover and simmer until meat is tender when pierced, about 2 to 2 ½ hours. Transfer pheasant to a warm serving platter, keep warm. Drink another glass of wine.

Boil pan juices over high heat. Sprinkle with 1 T flour, then whisk sour cream into pan juices. Cook, stirring, until heated through. Spoon sauce over individual servings. Finish the bottle.

Serve with wild rice. Makes 4 servings. Open another bottle of wine for the "guests."

Out of respect for the spirit of the birds, I wanted to make use of them as much as possible, so I decided to make the stunningly beautiful pelts of the males into hats (the hens were too drab). I chose three of the most breathtaking pelts for their iridescent colors of green and bronze and black and gold. I salted the skin side of the pelts thickly with coarse kosher salt. Salt kills off any bacteria that may be festering on the fleshy side of the skin that has been exposed. Also, salt dehydrates the flesh and blocks further growth of bacteria by eliminating moisture.

I draped the salted pelts skin-side down over overturned mixing bowls. I left them to dry for about three weeks, salting them again a couple more times. The pelts dried into perfect head-size rounds. I found some felt caps that I stitched the feather pelts onto. The results were unbelievably gorgeous. I had three of the most beautiful feather hats in all the world. I was making plans to visit the sporting camp on a regular basis to scrounge the left behind birds to make into chapeaus. I could sell these in Manhattan in a heartbeat!

I wore my pheasant hat all the time for about a month. I got tons of compliments—especially when I said I made it myself. One day, as I was wearing my hat, Tom was peering at me intently. I thought maybe he was thinking how beautiful I looked.

I asked coyly, "Are you bedazzled by my sheer beauty?"

He replied, "Ah, no, not exactly, honey. I'm pretty sure you are sporting a head full of maggots."

CROW FLIES HOME

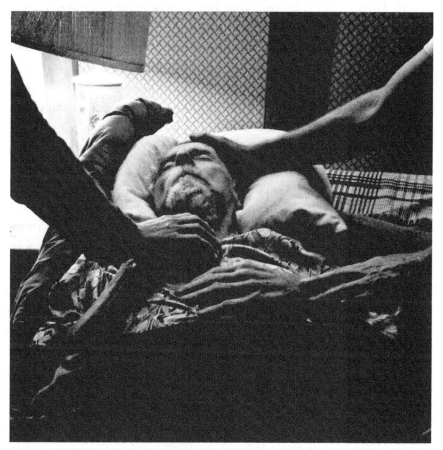

Dying Crow with his children

I've been thinking a lot about death lately and what happens after death. This past fall, I had the deep honor of midwifing my old friend, Crow

Dickinson, through the veil to the Otherside, gracefully in the dawning hours. Crow crossed over as windy skies cloaked the total lunar eclipse of the full Blood Moon. He died in his sweet little antique center-chimney Cape house on his mountaintop in the White Mountains of New Hampshire. I was honored to be his ending midwife.

A little backstory: here's why I loved Crow, and why I was so indebted to him. I first met Crow when he was an elder statesman who helped me immeasurably with New Hampshire legislation enabling midwives to practice freely in our state. He helped create our Board of Midwifery—in essence, he saved our collective butts. But what he really did was teach me the ropes, the ins and outs of the legislative process. He taught me so well that I eventually became a Lobbyist for the NH Midwives Association and was successful in winning insurance mandates for home births.

Crow could be, I guess I'd say, sardonic. Once when a pompous, vertically challenged, Napoleonic legislator was opposing us, Crow said, "That guy is so dumb, he has to unzip his pants to count to eleven."

Fast-forward 20 years later when Crow was diagnosed with end stage pancreatic cancer. His children really stepped up to the plate to take care of him in his last days in his home. This was momentous, because there had been years of neglect and abandonment of his children when Crow was in his "Glory Days." Nevertheless, his children took him home to care for him lovingly until the end. They asked me if I would help them. I said I would be honored to be his Deathing Midwife. As a midwife, the similar energies of birth and the entrance into this world and of death and the exit out of this world were very familiar to me.

Three days before Crow's death, I drove across the Kancamagus Highway through the notch in the White Mountains to get to his farm. It was a beautiful sunny day and the mountains were in their full blazing glory with peak fall foliage. When I got to Crow, I was impressed with how serene he seemed. His skin had a translucent, waxy appearance. He didn't acknowledge me, but when I asked him if he was in any pain, he said clearly, "No."

It took only minutes to realize his "serenity" was due to renal failure.

Over the course of a couple of days, Crow got increasingly agitated and restless. He was very weak and needed assistance getting in and out of bed, but he insisted on thrashing around, stripping off his beautiful silk brocade kimonos that he had had handmade for him in years gone by. He was irritable and bossy with us, but didn't seem to be fearful. I was considering giving him a heavy dose of the Ativan that the hospice nurse had left for anxiety—but for some reason, I didn't.

I'm so very glad we didn't drug him because we would have missed the miracle that came next.

Crow had been unable to get out of his bed for over a day when all of a sudden he *roared* up and said, "I have to climb the mountain!" He bounded out of bed, grabbed hold of his walker and stormed off stark naked down the hall to the kitchen, his pendulous scrotum swaying as he walked. I was trailing after him in case he fell. Crow was a tall man, at least 6'5", and once upon a time larger than life. I realized then that he had packed an incredible amount of living into that giant body of his, but now as I "hiked the mountain" with him; his frame seemed gaunt and strangely fragile.

He strode into the old kitchen, but I could see he was starting to falter. There was a stunning view of snowy Mount Washington from his kitchen window.

I yelled, "You did it, Crow! You've reached the summit! You're at the Observatory!"

He threw his head back and pumped his fist in the air in triumph and howled, "I did it! I climbed the mountain!"

Then I turned his walker around and he stomped back to the sunroom. He barely got to his bedside when he started to collapse, so I parked his butt on the edge of the bed and flipped his long legs up just as he lost all momentum.

Then he looked directly at me, his eyes filling with recognition. *"YOU!?"* He was completely lucid. "What are you doing here?"

I answered, "I'm midwifing you, Crow."

"You are? Why?"

"Because you're dying."

"I am?"

"Yes, all of your vital organs are shutting down as we speak."

"Oh…shit."

Then he turned to his daughter, Anne: "And *YOU!* What are *you* doing here?"

Anne said, "Same thing, Dad. I just came from Santa Fe."

Crow muttered, "Well, how about that."

This was twelve hours before his death.

Then he became very peaceful and calm. Anne went outside and brought in a handful of beautiful, colorful fall leaves. Crow lay placidly playing with them, staring at the colors, repeatedly folding and unfolding them, like Origami. He seemed content and quiet and completely engrossed in the vibrant leaves.

At one point, he looked out the window and saw his adult son, Alex, whom they still called "Mouse," in the yard. Mouse was building an amazing, crazy, art deco chicken coop out of twisted cedar trunks.

Crow said, "Who is that?"

162

I answered, "It's Mouse. He's building a chicken coop."

Crow looked startled, "So, he's here, too? That's amazing." That was the last thing he ever said. Then he seemed to slip away on his journey, wherever it is that we go. He never did regain consciousness. The "death rattle" began soon after that. I gave him oral morphine, and perhaps that speeded the process, I don't know. It came quicker than I thought it would.

When he stopped his last labored breath, I realized what a good home death he'd had and how incredibly important this was. I was proud of him. The scientific axiom came to my mind: "Energy is neither created nor destroyed. Energy changes form." Radical transformation. And so it did. Looking at my friend's face frozen open-mouthed in death was the saddest joy I have ever known.

Crow's children wrote a priceless and ribald obituary for him, the last sentence of which reads: "Be sure to be nice to your children, because in the end, they are the ones who hold your hand when you are dying and then—they write your obituary."

GODSPEED YOU ON YOUR NEW JOURNEY, DEAR OLD CROW!

SKINNER HARRIS

Skinner Harris Ilsley

I was driving down Dimond Hill at dusk to go to the evening shift at the Health Center when I saw a dark-colored mink lying in the middle of the road. He must have been trying to get to Ash Brook when he was hit. I slammed on my brakes and pulled over, and made all the oncoming cars go around me as I stood over the still body, protecting it from getting injured further. It looked like the animal's spirit was still in its body, so I gently nudged it with the toe of my boot to avoid a nasty bite, if he was still capable. No response.

I leaned over and palpated a very faint heartbeat. He was still warm but his eyes were getting dim. His life force was leaving him. I scooped him up to get him out of traffic and put him in the back hatch of my Jeep. I sat stroking his silky fur. His body was perfect, no sign of trauma. He was a buck male with beautiful mahogany colored fur and a little "soul patch" of white fur under his chin. I had no idea what I was going to do with him, but I had to get to work. I left him gently curled up in a little nest of blankets in the back of my car.

The next morning I called a man whom I had met from the NH Trapper's Association to ask who could help me preserve this mink. He said none of the NH trappers skinned their own animals any more; they all brought them to a man in Weare for processing. I was astounded. All these macho trappers just caught their animals—but didn't clean them? What the hell? He said the man who did the skinning for *all* of New England was a guy named Harris Ilsley. He explained to me where he lived, because apparently Mr. Ilsley didn't believe in using the telephone.

I drove around Weare until I knew I was at the right address. The yard was littered with rusted-out trucks in varying degrees of dilapidation. There were numerous wooden buildings in sad states of disrepair, with blown out windows and blue tarps over leaking roofs. There were muddy ruts in the leftover snow leading to different shacks. But in all this squalor, rather surprisingly, there were several bird feeders and hives of honeybees, the remnants of a greenhouse and the skeleton of last summer's vegetable garden.

I parked in the ruts next to what I thought was probably the main house where someone could maybe survive the winter. I walked over rotting porch floorboards up to the door that was leaning on its hinges. I knocked on the door until I noticed it was closed with a screwdriver—from the outside—so Mr. Ilsley obviously was not within.

I walked up the lane to an outbuilding and stuck my head inside, calling, "Hullo? Anybody here?" That's when I noticed all the freezers—and the blood on the floor. I was getting pretty sketched out at this point. I had no idea what Mr. Ilsley would be like—or if he'd be delighted to see me. Just then I remembered that I hadn't told Tom what I was doing. I called him on his cell phone. I left a voice-mail telling him that if I wasn't home for dinner it was because I was in a freezer in Weare.

I could feel someone watching me, but there wasn't a sound. I got back in my car and sat for a few minutes. I really did need to do something with this poor mink. I drove out of the yard and across the road to a gas station/convenience store. I asked the guys there if they knew if Mr. Ilsley was home. They shook their heads. They said they hadn't seen him in over a decade. They also said that if Mr. Ilsley didn't know me, he wouldn't come out.

Damn it. I drove back in the yard and got out of my car. I was standing in the sun and now I could *really* feel someone watching me. I looked around at all the wooden structures until I saw a slight movement. I couldn't believe my eyes. Standing next to an apple tree was a little leprechaun—a little man with a porkpie hat, smoking a curved pipe. He was peering at me intently.

"Mr. Ilsley?" I walked through the snow toward him. He didn't move. He just kept puffing on his pipe.

I stuck out my hand. "I got your name from the NH Trappers because I have a mink that needs to be skinned."

His eyes grew wide and he broke into a grin. His teeth looked like a NASCAR checkered flag.

"Oh Jesus, deah. I thought you were one of them anti's."

He gestured for me to follow him inside a big unpainted building. At this point I was wondering…anti? Anti what? …Anti-choice? Anti-women's reproductive rights? Where am I right now? Oh…anti-*TRAPPING!* I get it now, another beleaguered and misunderstood, marginalized group.

When I crossed the threshold into the building, I stood stock-still. I felt as though I had crossed over into the early 18th century. When my eyes adjusted to the dimmer light, I realized I was standing in a big barn-like workroom that had hundreds and hundreds of fur pelts hanging from hooks from the roof rafters. Coyotes and fox and raccoons. Row upon row of beautiful lush fur pelts.

Along the far wall were stacks of skinned beavers, pink and white carcasses. I only knew they were beavers because of the big flat black tails that were still attached to the bodies, about fifty tails hanging down in the pile. Alongside the beavers were skinned coyote carcasses with their teeth leering menacingly. In front of us were huge round wooden pallets for stretching beaver and otter pelts. The beavers that were already dried were stacked in row after row of round pelts that had been removed from the wooden spheres. At our feet were many more animals—still intact—waiting for Mr. Ilsley. There must have been over a thousand dead animals in this place.

Harris at work

As my eyes became focused in the gloom, I absorbed more of the 18th century I found myself standing in. There were crates full of discarded entrails, and congealed blood inches thick on the floor. Decades of blood. Mr. Ilsley walked over to a small table that had two soda fountain stools in front of it, sat down and re-lit his pipe. He puffed a few times, still eyeing me warily. I'm sure he thought I was from PETA and I was going to scream and douse him with fake blood at any minute.

He asked, "You a midwife?"

"How'd you know that?"

He nodded toward the door, "Your car's tags."

"Oh, right!" I grinned. "Yes, actually, you might know the old country doctor who trained me, Doctor Francis Brown from Henniker. He was the one who taught me my trade thirty-seven years ago." I thought maybe Mr. Ilsley would know Francis, as Henniker was the next town over from Weare.

Harris let out a huge belly laugh and slapped his knee. "Doc Brown! He was my mother's doctor!" He wiped his eyes. "Ain't thet sumpthin!"

I was in like Flynn.

Now Harris became very animated and talkative. "I remember one time my mother cut her leg and she was bleeding pretty good. Doc Brown made a house call and patched up her leg." He took a long puff and then continued with his story. "Doc Brown told her if she ever cut her leg again to do this, and then Doc Brown *laid on the floor and stuck his leg straight up in the air.* Can you imagine a doctor today *lying on the floor?!?*" Harris was practically yelling at this point he was so excited.

I looked around at the present bloody floor. "Nope, I can't say I can think of a single doctor who would lie on the floor as a demonstration."

After this, Harris pretty much didn't stop talking the entire time I was hanging out with him. He agreed to skin my little boy mink for the hefty fee of $2.00. I sat next to him at the little table as he began skinning my mink. He started at the back foot and cut up toward the tail. He talked the whole time. As he deftly worked with a surprisingly small knife, he told me that he was born in 1930 and grew up on this farm in Weare, and had pretty much stayed close to home his whole life. When he was five years old, he had his own laying hens and sold his eggs on the side of the road. Then he started selling worms for bait to fishermen. He raised pigeons to sell the meat as squab.

Harris struggled a bit getting the tail skinned, but he finally got it freed. I have a great photo I took of him at that moment with a huge, triumphant grin. He continued his saga. He left school in the eighth grade because, he said, school for him was "poison." He started fishing and trapping along the local rivers. He learned to skin and care for the pelts very early on.

Next we moved over to a hook that was hanging from a rafter where he slowly pulled my mink inside out. I sat on a little leprechaun stool next to him. As he worked slicing the fascia and separating skin from muscle, he told me he did a fair amount of "hellin" around in his youth, but he never married. He worked hard and supported himself by gathering apple drops all over Weare and pressing them into cider. He kept hives of honeybees, and also hunted wild bees for honey. He grew potatoes, collected sap for maple syrup, and sold cords of firewood.

Harris put my mink on a ski-shaped drying board with a belly board to prevent the mink from sticking. He sat in front of the board where he "split the tail." He made sure I watched his technique. He said he skins more animals in a year than most trappers will do in a lifetime. He skins whatever comes in the door. Generally, Harris skins about 3,000 animals a year, and about 2,000 of those are beavers.

As the last step he skillfully "pleated" the tail with a dozen pushpins. He said most skinners don't bother to do this, but he believes this enhances the grade and gives the pelt a more luxurious "viewing area," as he called the finished product of the fur. Somehow our conversation wandered to Benson's Wild Animal Farm, a place we both had nostalgic memories of visiting as children. Harris told me he always had to ride with his teacher when they did the annual field trip to Benson's, as he was famous for getting carsick. He said it was an undisputed fact that if he took the bus, they would have to pull over to the side of the road several times so young Harris could yack.

"Pleating" the tail with push-pins

As I was leaving, Harris said he wanted to show me something. Way in the back recess of the skinning building were dozens of large cardboard boxes. Each box held several exquisitely hand-carved songbirds created by Harris. Each bird was lovingly carved and painted to be almost lifelike. I was astounded by their beauty. My favorite was a mother wood thrush with a worm in her mouth feeding the four wide-open, outstretched mouths of her hungry little nestlings.

"How long before my mink is ready to go home?" I asked.

"Oh, it'll only be about a week, deah."

I smiled. Good. I get to see Harris again in only seven days.

WHY I DECIDED TO TRAP BEAVERS

Beavah Diva!

When I was a young girl, my mother arranged for me to be able to tag along with old Doc Kennard of Bedford, NH. Doc Kennard was kind of famous as a naturalist/surgeon and he had a bird-banding station at his house that I helped him out with after school. At least, I thought he was famous, because he wrote many articles in bird-banding journals, such as: *Reverse migration in the Dark-eyed Junco.* Anyway, he was a wealth of knowledge, and he taught me how to identify bird calls and to track animal and bird tracks in the snow, and how to identify scat. He also removed my appendix.

I was a free-range kid. I was in love with the outdoors and built many "camps" in the woods where I set up small snare traps. I would camp out at my trap-lines overnight. I never caught anything, not sure I knew what I would do if I did find something in my snare. Actually, that's not true. I did once catch a vole but it got away because it bit me. I still have a crescent shaped scar on my right thumb.

Most people automatically assume that I am a vegetarian. I have no idea why. Even as a young kid, I craved protein. While my younger siblings would be delighting in sweet treats, I would go straight for the leftover hunk of steak in the fridge. My sibs would be wallowing in chocolate pudding and I would be smeared with A-1 Steak Sauce.

I did go through a spell of vegetarianism in my late teens, as being macrobiotic was all the rage. By the time I was down to about 100 pounds, my hair began falling out and my periods stopped and I realized I had to embrace my Inner Carnivore. The migraines ceased with my first cheeseburger.

As an adult woman, my diet preference was fish with occasional poultry and no "red meat." By the time menopause hit, the migraines were back with a vengeance. I realized I needed to embrace my Inner Carnivore once again. I craved all things red. It was a little scary. I became like Rosemary's Baby.

But back to trapping. Tom likes to hunt, and our land provides us with 400 acres of prime hunting. I, however, don't have a good history with guns. There was that very, *very* bad incident thirty-one years ago with a 12-gauge shotgun that did not end well. But I'm fine with trapping. And eviscerating. Tom is fine with killing but he developed a mild allergy to eviscerating. Thanks to my course in Field Dressing Big Game, I am totally comfortable with cleaning out entrails and now I can help him out. (When we did in our 12 roosters that were originally sold to us as "pullets," I found that I *love* having my hands in a still warm animal. It must be the midwife in me.)

I like the idea of harvesting our own food. Tom and I are at a point in our lives where we would like to know the origins of the food we eat, as much as possible, especially meat. I would like to reduce the amount of commercially raised meat that we consume; the more we can avoid the hormones and antibiotics of supermarket meat, the better. Our dream is to provide as much sustenance from our own land as possible. We have about 100 beavers flooding our farm right now. Beavers have the highest concentration of protein of all the animals and are considered by some to be a gourmet delicacy. I want our beavers to be a sustainable, renewable source of protein for us.

And I want them in my freezer.

Postscript: Carol ultimately did apprentice with two seasoned New Hampshire trappers. One very experienced, life-long trapper was an older gentleman named Mutton Chop. The other trapper was a fearless Algonquin Native American woman trapper named Bonnie.

Carol got her NH Trappers license when she was in her early 60's and Tom got his a year later. They have been eating beaver ever since.

How to Eat a Beaver

Carol's first beaver, "The Sentry," 55 lbs.

Since my decision to become a beaver eater, I have received a fair amount of criticism. One (former) Facebook friend even called me "Satanic" for wanting to eat these adorable, smart rodents. Here's my reasoning: I don't want to eat meat from the supermarkets anymore. The genetically modified "chickens" are a scientific horror story. These "birds" are featherless and, by 12 weeks of age, their breasts are so heavy that they can't walk and they have to crawl to their food. Big fat globs of featherless, wingless poultry meat crawling on the floor for food. Appalling. And now, with the expose' of "pink slime," ammonium hydroxidetreated meat in all the news; this just reinforces my determination to try to provide as much protein by our own means as possible.

I told my self-righteous, judgmental Facebook critics that unless they were total vegans and didn't support the US meat industry and if they didn't wear leather shoes, belts or man-purses—to back off and never give me flack about this again.

A week after I brought my little mink to be skinned, I went back to my new friend, Harris, to pick it up. I walked into Harris's big work space, and there he was, sitting on a little stool, almost lost amidst all the hanging coyote and fox pelts. He was working on a beaver that was hanging from a large hook in the ceiling. He was busy skillfully removing the pelt from the carcass with his knife. He still had on his little pork-pie hat, and the pipe was firmly clamped in his mouth.

I said, "Hi, Harris! Did you miss me?"

He looked up from his dangling carcass and gave me a huge checkered grin. I think he was truly glad to see me.

He said, "Well! If it isn't the Hippie Girl!"

Harris is a little, wiry old guy. He was wearing an old grimy, insulated long underwear top underneath a brand new-looking turquoise Izod Lacoste sport shirt. Spotless. And about three sizes too big. This cracked me up.

"You're looking stylish today, Harris."

There was a little low wooden stool right next to the one he was sitting on. It looked like a little kid's stool. I sat down next to him to watch him deftly cutting the fascia between muscle and skin.

He said, "Be careful. I think there's blood on that stool."

I said, "Harris, I think I've been sitting on bloody stools of one sort or another for over thirty-five years now."

He laughed out loud at that. "Oh, that's right. I forgot that blood wouldn't really bother you."

He told me that this was the peak of the beaver trapping season, as it ends on April 10th. He said the trappers were bringing in between 30 and 40 beavers a day for him to skin. He charged $4.00 an animal. There were about 20 beavers lying on their backs on the floor. I asked him if the beaver he was working on was fresh. He said it had come in from New Boston the day before. I asked him if I could have it to eat. He grinned at me.

"Sho-ah!" He almost shouted he was so pleased. "I'll just clean out the innards for you."

Harris didn't usually eviscerate the animals. He stretched the pelts on big wooden rounds and left the intact furless carcasses to pile up until they became a nuisance. Then he dragged them out to the top of a hill in back of his property for the coyotes and other scavengers to feast on. I was trying not to imagine what this place must smell like in the heat of summer. He said that every once in a while, the Health Department paid him a visit. I said, "I bet they do."

My beaver was a medium size female, probably about forty pounds. Harris quickly pulled out all the glistening blue and white entrails. I couldn't believe how *huge* they looked to me. The innards looked much bigger than a deer's. He asked me if I wanted the liver and I said, "Sure." The liver looked about the size of a dark crimson football. Harris removed the head and the tail and handed me the body. I put her in a new white garbage bag. The body was about three feet long and weighed a *lot*.

I was sitting on the tiny wooden stool next to Harris. I had the body-bagged beaver resting in my lap. He turned to me and said very gently, "I started reading your book the other night. It seems like you had some real pain in your younger years—that you're no stranger to sorrow."

My eyes welled up with tears at his empathy. "Yeah, I had a pretty rough go of it for a while there." I sighed. Then the irony of me being consoled by a bloody little leprechaun who was sitting in front of a dangling, naked beaver carcass made me smile. "But I'm good now, Harris, honest—my life is good."

He nodded and puffed on his pipe. We continued chatting. I think we wandered into a discussion about the widespread use of anti-depressants, which he disdained. Harris also told me about his infamous stint raising mink years ago, to sell for their fur. He fed his mink the leftover beaver carcasses. He said the mink *loved* beaver meat. They loved the beaver meat so much they got fat and lazy and refused to mate. They had absolutely no interest in reproducing, so Harris's mink farming enterprise was a bust.

[Note to self: Be careful how much beaver meat I feed Tom.]

Our pleasant exchange was interrupted when a trapper came in to hire Harris's services. I said goodbye to my talkative friend and pecked him on the cheek. I picked up my girl beaver and walked past the trapper to go out the door.

The trapper's mouth was agape. I heard him ask, "Jesus, what the hell was that?"

What I have since found out is, although many trappers claim that beaver meat is delicious, no one I spoke with had actually cooked one. Even the acclaimed wild game chef who wrote the cookbook *Cook Wild New Hampshire* for the Fish & Game Department had never actually butchered a beaver. I soon realized I was on my own.

So I did the most common-sense thing to do. I called my friend Kendall.

Kendall and I have a long history of foraging for wild food together—mushroom hunting, fishing, the occasional (still warm) road-killed wild turkeys. I knew this would be perfectly understandable to her. I was right. Kendall brought over a half gallon of white wine and we dug right in.

Harris had already removed the castor glands from this beaver. He sells them for their scent–he told me castor is the base for Channel #5! He cautioned me to remove the fat near the hind legs as there were two more, smaller scent glands in that fat that could taint the meat. Kendall and I set up a cleaning station outside in the driveway and began what turned out to be a fascinating anatomy lesson. We each had a skinning knife. Carefully exploring our beaver to find the meat that was acceptable, we got into a rhythm, Kendall removing fat and me feeling for the fine textured red meat.

Here's what we got...I got two long back-straps from both sides of the backbone, which were wider at the shoulders and tapered to a point near the tail. Kendall wrestled a large amount of meat from the hams; the large muscles attesting to the powerful back legs and tail of our beaver. I found two tenderloins inside the body cavity in about the middle of the beaver and to either side of the backbone. The meat wasn't pretty. It was obviously a hack job, but in the end, we had about five pounds of strips of fresh New Hampshire beaver.

I get such a kick out of Kendall. She's the product of New England girls' boarding schools, which she rejected heartily in the 1960s. Now we were sitting together, hunched over our first beaver, our fingers exploring. It made me grin to see her daintily sip from her glass of Chardonnay—with rivers of beaver blood trailing down her arm to her elbow. That's true friendship right there, by gawd.

We were just finishing up when a young couple showed up for a visit. The young husband was looking for Tom, who had very conveniently left on a motorcycle outing with his brother, leaving Kendall and me on our own to do the dirty work. The couple looked *very* skeeged out, and I realized this must be one of the most hillbilly things they had ever laid eyes on. We invited them to dinner, but they politely declined.

I decided I wanted to cook the beaver without much additional seasoning, as I wanted to get a real idea of what the unadorned meat tasted like. No marinating. I floured the beaver meat by putting a couple of cups of flour in a large Ziploc bag, adding the meat and shaking it. Then we simply pan-fried it in extra virgin olive oil in a large skillet and stood around drinking wine as we watched it cook. It hadn't cooked for very long before I thought it looked done and I had to try it.

With some trepidation I put the first morsel in my mouth. I could not believe the sensation in my mouth. It was more of an experience than a taste. SWEET BEAVER! It was absolutely incredible. I think my eyes glazed over in ecstasy. It tasted *fresh* like spring and clean fresh water, a little minty like alders and poplar trees—not gamey *at all*. I was tasting the habitat of my wild beaver. It was delicious and tender and mild all at once. Actually, it didn't taste like "meat," certainly not the mealy crap they're selling in the grocery stores.

Beavers are vegetarians, existing mostly on deciduous trees. In the right environment, they are living in fresh water away from pollutants and chemicals. The only way I could explain what it tastes like when people asked if it was like chicken or pork, was to compare it to the difference between a store bought tomato and one straight from your garden. There is simply no way to compare the experience of the two tastes.

I bet that when the fur traders came to North America and started trapping beavers for their pelts, they threw the meat away, just like what happened to the buffalo. Buffalo hides were prized, but the carcasses of the animals were left in huge mountains to rot. Heartbreaking waste. People assumed that the meat was inedible. Even today, beaver pelts are prized and are big sellers in China, but the meat is discarded. The Native Americans considered beaver to be a delicacy. Now I know they were right.

A little later after our test-tasting, Tom and his brother, Lee, returned from their motorcycle ride.

I asked his brother, "Hey, Lee, do you want to taste my beaver?"

He said, "Nope. No thanks. Nah, I'm good."

**Tom with a gorgeous red-pelted "ginger beaver"
in Hopkinton, NH ~ Winter 2014.**

BEAVER TRAPPING FIELD NOTES, PART I

The far dam at Beavertown in Hopkinton, NH

Saturday, 6:00 PM

Overcast, foggy, drizzly.

Tom and I set 2 Conibear 330s in two active swales leading to the lower beaver pond dam.* We had a long discussion but decided to put the dog (trigger wires) up from the bottom. We staked the Conibears securely with four stakes. Baited with "Popple" (Big-tooth aspen, Populus grandidentata—see illustration). Will check traps early in the AM.

*I have to confess right here that I'm not strong enough to set a Conibear with my bare hands. Tom can do it easily, but I just don't have enough strength in my hands to compress the springs and powerful jaws. I got a setting tool that makes it so much easier. Even so, I have to use my thighs to compress the setting tool. I've found this is making my thighs much more taut, therefore, I call the setting tool "The Thigh Master." This would be very sexy except the setting tool leaves a brutal line of black and blue bruises up and down my inner thighs. How enticing is that?

I swear I heard the beavers laughing at me.

Sunday, 7:00 AM

Rainy, windy, totally shitty.

Nothing. One trap sprung, probably triggered by something small that swam right through…muskrat? Tom re-set. We will dismantle part of the dam today to get them back working these swales tonight.

Sunday, 6:00 PM

Still daylight, went by myself.

Slogged through about 2 feet of cold water that is flooding our field. Muckboots filled almost immediately. Slipped and fell face first in a deep water-filled rut. The beavers are still laughing. Checked traps—nothing. Still set and undisturbed. We had a bunch of visitors today so didn't get around to tearing down the dam. I wonder if I should bait with APPLES?

Monday, 7:00 AM

Sunny and nice (got a photo of a really beautiful dew laced spider's web on a tree).

Traps EMPTY. As I was leaning down to look at footprints in the mud a Red-winged Blackbird (Agelaius phoeniceus) was screaming at me. The bird was definitely flitting from branch to branch to get a closer look at what I was doing. All the while it kept screaming a bird rendition of ALERT! Finally it landed on a branch right in front of my face. He looked right at me and I knew then I was busted. That damn bird absolutely knew I was up to no-good and was a predator. He outed my nefariousness. He wasn't a Red-winged Blackbird—he was a Stool Pigeon! He screamed again full of warning and swooped low over the beaver pond. I heard a loud SLAP! and a splash as all the beavers raced away…laughing.

We've got to lower the dam today to get them back over on this (NW) side of the pond.

Monday, 6:00 PM

Pleasant and mild.

OK, I'll be honest. At this point I'm just hanging out in the swamp enjoying the raw beauty of nature. We didn't get around to messing with the dam today as Tom is busy in the woods getting in our winter firewood. He's taken to singing an annoying little ditty that goes something like:

"Oh, my wife thought she was going to DECEIVE A BEAVAH—but instead they heaved her beeve." Har-dee-har, Tommy.

Next weekend I'm going to make fake "scent mounds" by forming a pile of mud and putting Castor scent (their strong territorial scent) on top for a lure.

Tuesday, 7:00 AM

Blindingly sunny.

Nuthin. Traps still set. Not only that…but every scrid of Popple bait is GONE! Even the saplings that we used to hold the traps in place have been chewed right down to the ground. The first swale is very muddy and the water level is high. There are beaver tracks, carrying their heavy flat tails, all around the sets. In beaver language, this is definitely, "Na na nuh doodie."

I sprang both traps with a stake to bring them back with me. The traps were not as trigger-happy as I anticipated. It was hard to snap them—but the *power of the jaws when they did snap made me feel a little faint. I think next time I'll put the dog (trigger wires) at the top.*

This beaver trapping business is not going to be as easy as I thought. I'm beginning to feel like Wile E. Coyote.

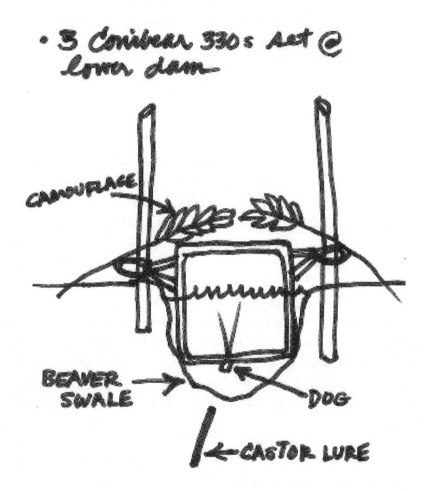

First illustration of setting up a Conibear 330 from field notes.

My Discovery

I think I've made a discovery about the rarity of consuming beaver meat. I think I've figured out why beaver meat has such a bad rap. Most trappers I know scorn it...old time trappers won't touch it and say it's inedible and tastes "like a dog's breakfast." How could this be when I found it to be a delicacy? When I was dreaming about having a freezer full of the stuff? Something was askew.

One day I was trapping with Mutton Chop when he said we had to use a leg-hold trap because this particular beaver that he was nuisance trapping had become "Conibear shy"—this means the beaver probably got "snapped" by the jaws of a Conibear but not killed—which created a beaver that would forever avoid anything shaped like a steel square. Mutton Chop set the leg-hold trap on top of the dam and we left it for the night.

The next morning, sure enough, there was a beaver in the leg-hold trap—and that beaver *was not happy*. Mutton Chop walked up to him and shot him in the head. I made a mental note right then to only use Conibear 330s when trapping, as this is an "instant kill" trap and seems so much more humane. The beavers never even know what hit them.

I took that beaver home with me to skin and prepare it for Tom for that night's dinner. I butchered it exactly the same way I had done all the others, being careful not to nick the castor glands. But when I put the backstrap in the cast iron frying pan to cook it—the gagging stench of castor was so overwhelming, I had to throw it out. My eyes were watering from the fumes. It *was* inedible.

Here's what I deduced after comparing the background of this beaver vs. the previous ones I had cooked. The only difference in the treatment was the trap. The leg-hold trap gave the beaver time to taint the meat with adrenaline, much the same way venison can be ruined by a deer that runs after a misplaced shot and is chased. Stress causes adrenaline to be secreted into the blood streams of these animals and makes the meat unpalatable.

The Conibear trap was invented in 1956 as a more humane way to harvest fur. So that means that old time trappers who were trapping prior to this time experienced the stanky results of stress-tainted meat. They were the ones who gave beaver meat a bad reputation—and they were right. But with a Conibear trapped beaver, you are getting the unadulterated animal. Beavers are vegetarian. They eat poplar and aspen and they live in fresh, clean flowing water so they taste like that—they taste light and fresh and healthy. They taste like Spring.

SAVE A TREE ... EAT A BEAVER!

NO BEER AND SQUIRREL HOT WINGS

"I can't do this." I am trying to make the first incision along the inside of a squirrel's hind leg. I find I simply cannot. I strip off my vinyl gloves and grab a new pair and hand them to Tom. "Here, you do it."

Tom has been standing at my shoulder, watching. He puts on the new gloves and deftly makes the first cut, then begins to peel back the "silver skin" as the hunters call the fascia. His motions are sure, like a surgeon's.

I'm surprised that I balked at this. I have to admit I was a little shocked when we walked out of the hunting lodge and there were a couple dozen dead gray squirrels lined up on the picnic tables, ready to be "skunned" by the participants—the erstwhile "Wild Game Culinary Chefs." The wanna-be chefs here are pumped to dig into some wild game. It's like gourmet cooking on steroids. Julia Child dressed in camo, "Bon Appetit… ya'll!"

Lately, I've been apprenticing with an older gentleman, a skilled master trapper whom I call Mutton Chop because of his huge white sideburns. I've been riding around with Mutton Chop trapping destructive wild animals for the DOT. I know when I slide out of the "Nuisance Wildlife Control" truck trailing after Mutton Chop, the people who have hired him to dust their pests look squinting out of their eyes sideways at me, wondering if I'm his girlfriend. Mutton Chop wears a big Bowie knife hanging from his belt. I started wearing a culinary fillet knife in a leather holster hanging from my belt so people will know I'm not Mutton Chop's girlfriend, dammit, I'm a friggin' bad-ass *TRAPPERETTE*.

I've skinned a bunch of beavers under Mutton Chop's direction without hesitation, and their meat is delicious. While I admire and respect beavers for their incredible ingenuity and persistence and I *do* find them adorable and smart—the reality is they are flooding over 50 acres of our prime real estate, so those cute rodents have got to go—straight into my freezer.

Now this flaccid "wild game" in my hands has been capped in the ass by a twelve-year-old boy out squirrel hunting with his buddies. The hind end is full of lead #7 birdshot. I stroke the fur gently. I turn the squirrel over to check out the anatomy and discover it is a female. Ah, so here's where the hesitation comes from…

…another little girl squirrel cavorts into my memory.

When I was 20 years old, some neighbor kids brought me a baby gray squirrel to tend to. A local boy had shot the mother squirrel in her nest and all the other babies died except for this one. I was a Natural History major in college at the time, so I consulted with my professors about the best way to care for this feeble female newborn squirrel. I ended up feeding her a concoction of yogurt and mashed oatmeal from an eyedropper. She began to get stronger and to grow. Actually, by the time this squirrel was a year old, she was huge. She was bigger than a house cat.

I named her Bourgeois. I have no idea where that came from or why; I certainly didn't speak French. I called her Boojie for short. I fell madly in love with this animal and cared for her as anyone would for their pet. My house, which was an old Grange Hall in Bradford at the time, became full of stashes of walnuts and cranberries under every pillow and in every crevice. When Boojie was extremely happy or startled, she would do a back flip straight up in the air. She was very playful and sometimes naughty—like when she would run up my body like a tree trunk and frantically dig in my head for no apparent reason.

I remember the time I took Boojie to Saint Louis to visit my girlfriend, Nancy, who used to be my freight train hopping partner. Boojie and I went to Missouri from New Hampshire on a BUS. I have no idea what I was thinking, but I hid Boojie in a fancy hatbox and off we went on an overnight bus ride. Boojie was pretty good until the middle of the night when she made it very clear she was getting pissed at being confined in such a small space for so long. It was quiet and dark on the bus, so I put Boojie on a leash and let her run back and forth up above on the luggage rack.

Unfortunately, a bleached-blonde woman in the seat in front of us woke up and saw what probably looked like a giant rat running above her head. This woman had on more eye-makeup than Tammy Faye Baker… which accented her eyeballs as they grew huge and she was about to scream. I quickly covered her mouth and told her that it was my pet. She looked at me like I was a freaking madwoman and she continued to track my girl's movement out of the corner of her heavily mascara-caked eye—but she didn't bust me by complaining to the driver.

When we got to Saint Louis, the city was experiencing a deadly heat wave. I was assigned to stay in the third floor garret apartment of Nancy's parents' brick house. It was so stifling hot up there that I spent a great deal of the time soaking in a large claw foot bathtub, drinking gin and tonics. Boojie was so hot she got peevish and growly. I gave her ice cubes, which she would lick and then turn the cube around and around in her paws like she did with walnuts. She loved those ice cubes. She loved them so much that she stashed them all under a pillow.

Boojie spent a lot of the time lying—spread-eagled—next to me along the cool porcelain rim of the tub. She was panting. Me too. We were from New England, so this sultry heat was kicking the snot out of us both. When Booj got too hot she ran to the pillow to retrieve her ice cubes. She dug further under the pillow, and when she discovered they were gone she turned to me and started chattering at me full blast with what I can only imagine were the worse cuss words that a squirrel could come up with. When I started laughing at her, that only made her madder. She was ripshit. She ran back and glared at my glass, which was full of the ice cubes that she knew I had stolen from her. It was the only time I was actually afraid that she might bite me.

When Boojie reached sexual maturity she got bitchy and moody—like any other pubescent female. She started hibernating in the fiberglass insulation in the attic of the Grange. She got testy and screamed at me when I pulled her down—kind of equivalent, I guess, to a 14 year old girl calling you an asshole and slamming the door to her bedroom and staying in there for days. It was when Boojie started chewing the electrical wiring that I admitted she was depressed and needed to be re-introduced into the wild.

I re-introduced her slowly. I had a little land-locked cabin in Newbury that overlooked the backside of Mount Sunapee. I took Boojie there and we camped out for the remainder of the summer into early fall. We took long walks in the woods. At first Boojie stayed pretty close to me, running high above in the trees but always coming when I called. Then I left her for a few days at a time. Every time I returned I would call to her, and within a few minutes a huge gray squirrel would gleefully pounce on my shoulder, sniffing my neck in greeting. It was breaking my heart, but I knew that she was adapting well.

The waiting time it took for her to return to me got longer and longer and longer—until, finally, she didn't return at all.

Now I am surrounded by huge men dressed all in camo down to their skivvies. They are studiously skinning the squirrels to get the legs cleaned to be cooked tonight like chicken hot wings. Seriously? When the legs are all cleaned up they look about the size of a pathetic frog's leg.

These are the guys who drove me out in the middle of the night, into the dark unknown. I forgot what it was like to sleep with a bunch of large, sleep apneic men, the snoring sounds like competing bullfrogs.

"GARUM! Snort…snxzzt."

From the other side of the cabin, "GARUM! Snort…fart."

After several hours of this chainsaw massacre, I say, "F-this." I take my sleeping bag and pillow and drag myself out to my car. It is so peaceful, with the sound of a rushing brook nearby. Sigh. I'm so glad my years of being a midwife prepared me to love sleeping in my car. I spend the rest of the time bunking in the blissful quiet of a parking lot deep in the Northern woodlands.

Tonight's menu is the squirrel hot wings and roast moose. The squirrel legs come out slathered in red Frank's hot sauce. They have shrunk down to about the size of a Guinea pig leg. I watch as the huge men grab handfuls of the tiny legs and start crunching into the crispy critters. I take one little limb and bite with trepidation, trying my best not to think of Boojie. I immediately grind into a mouthful of lead birdshot which I discreetly spit into my camo-print paper napkin. BLECH! I'm pretty sure I can feel my brain cells dying from lead poisoning (and heaven only knows I can't afford to lose any more of those precious babies).

And to make matters worse, there is not a drop of beer to wash this all down with. Not a Smuttynose in sight. Good Godfrey! I say to the man sitting across the table from me, whose neck is thicker than my thigh, "I'm thinking about becoming a vegetarian right now."

He levels me with a steely, empty wolf-gaze. He growls, "Does not the carrot scream when it is ripped from the soil? And then the vegetarian eats it raw…sometimes right there, in front of the rest of the carrot family, with no concern whatsoever about the emotional impact on the rest of the row."

Okey dokey, pretty damn scary and point well taken. But…moose and squirrel? I've had it with this Rocky and Bullwinkle bullshit.

From now on I'm sticking strictly to beavers.

SUPER BEAVER MOON

It was after dark last night when I went to close the chickens in their coop. I opened the front door and, too late, I heard a coyote howl right in our front yard. Both of our dogs went charging off the porch in hot pursuit of the intruder. *SHIT!* I screamed "coyote!" to Tom but wasn't sure if he heard me. I went running down our road to the lower east field where all the commotion was.

Last night was the "super moon," actually it was the super *BEAVER* moon, so I was able to see pretty well once my eyes adjusted to the moonlight. When I got to the clearing by the beaver flowage, I saw two dark animals frantically patrolling back and forth along the perimeter of the forest, sniffing the ground and barking ferociously, protecting their territory. Then I realized there were more silhouettes of dark animals growling menacingly, coming closer out of the woods.

Alrighty then, probably *not* a good situation to be in lit up like a Christmas tree in the moonlight, standing there in my flimsy Sketcher slip-ons in the frost, screaming to my dogs. The growling and the barking and the frantic movements escalating until it was bedlam. Total chaos. My dogs were about to get in a gang fight with the wild dogs. The Jets and the Sharks. The Domestics and the Ferals. I knew for certain who would win this fight.

The barking and the howling and the growling increased, as did my screaming. It was reaching fever pitch. All of a sudden there was a loud **BLAM!** A gunshot. My mouth dropped open.

I turned to look back up our road. On top of the hill, standing in the moonlight, Tom was holding a rifle up in the air. He was standing in his muck boots and his pajama bottoms (his flannel Christmas jammies that have Santa riding on a motorcycle).

All noise ceased immediately. Our dogs came running back with a frantic look on their faces like, "Holy shit, man!" I wasn't sure if they were more freaked out about the potential gang war...or the fact that Tom had fired off a round in the air. Either way, they were ready to call it a night.

Then we closed in the chickens—all were accounted for—and went back into the house. I love my husband. The end.

SISTER FLO

I remember the first time I laid eyes on Flo. Looking back, it's interesting, because she showed up in my life right before Christmas in 1986, a month before my husband Ken died. Of course, I had no idea he was going to die. Just as I had no idea at the time about the significance of a black dog appearing mysteriously in my life—about the Celtic mythology that the black dog was a messenger from the Underworld, and that she would portend death.

I was returning home from my midwifery office and was turning into my snowy driveway when I saw, at the entrance to my drive, a medium size black dog sitting tensely erect and looking at me expectantly.

I lowered the passenger side window and said, in jest, "Oh, hello, have you been waiting for me long?"

The black dog wagged her tail tentatively. As I drove down the driveway, I looked in my rear-view mirror and saw her begin to trot and follow me down the drive.

When I opened the front door, the black dog shot past me, and ran upstairs and hid under my bed. I put groceries away, and then I went upstairs and lay on the floor, talking to her gently as she cowered under my bed.

"What's your story, my friend? What's your name? Do you have anyone who is missing you right now? It's okay, you don't need to be afraid."

Her tail bumped a nervous rhythm but she wouldn't come out. I gave her a couple of stale cookies that I found in the pantry.

When Ken came home, he went upstairs to try to get her to come out. She bared her fangs at him and growled ferociously. He called her a "cur"…among other things, mostly the "B" word. I lay down again and looked at her more closely. She was trembling beneath the undercarriage of the bed. She looked to be in fairly good health, although *very* skinny—her ribs desperately needed more flesh on them. But her eyes were clear and intelligent and—what? Something about her eyes riveted me.

I let her stay under the bed for the night, despite Ken's protestations. After Ken left for the hospital in the morning, I managed to get her to come out. I gave her a bowl of water, opened the front door and sent her on her way. I have to admit, I didn't really think too much about her after that.

A couple of days later, as I was driving to work, I saw the black dog in a neighboring field in the snow. I pulled over on the side of the road and watched her. It appeared that she was playing. She would cock her head sideways, looking intently at the snow, then leap up in the air, slam her paws down, and bury her whole snout in the snow. When she surfaced, she

194

had a *mouse* in her mouth that she swallowed in one gulp. Ah! I had seen coyotes do this—hearing their meals scurrying under the crust of the snow.

The black dog saw me watching her. She came over to my car and cocked one eyebrow. I got out as if it was customary and opened the back door like a chauffeur, and she jumped in. What can I say? I certainly hadn't planned on adopting a feral dog. But the black dog sat regally in the back seat of my car as though it was her throne, placidly looking out the window.

I convinced Ken that someone would certainly claim such an obviously intelligent dog, so he allowed her in the house while I contacted the police and the local pound. Nobody had reported a lost dog. The more I looked at her, the more I was convinced that she had been on the road for a long, *long* time. I didn't tell Ken that. I put a "Found Dog" ad in the local papers. A young couple responded and said she matched the description of their lost dog. They came into the house eagerly, but the woman's face crumpled when she saw that the black dog was not theirs. She started sobbing as though her heart were breaking.

"I'm really very sorry that I got your hopes up," I said to the couple. It was starting to dawn on me that I was about to have a new dog.

Ken was actually the one who named her. He was standing behind her and said loudly, "Who are you? Are you Muffy?"

No response.

"Are you Fifi?"

Nothing.

"Are you Flo?" With this the black dog whipped her head around and looked at Ken with clear recognition. Florence. Really?

It seemed incongruous to name a semi-wild dog after the matriarch of the Brady Bunch—but Flo it was. It was the name she answered to for the rest of her life.

I brought Flo to my friend Jim Paine, the local veterinarian, to be checked out. Jim said he thought she was around five years old and seemed to be in good health, despite being on her own for who knows how long. He said she appeared to be a terrier, mixed with—what? Perhaps coyote. A terrier-coyote hybrid. Jim also believed that Flo had been spayed, as she had no obvious signs of having had litters.

I let Flo come and go as she liked. I left the sliding glass door open just enough for her to squeeze through to the unheated, back sun porch, where I put a dog bed down for her. In the beginning, she would be gone for several days, so I didn't know if she would ever be coming back or not. But then, there'd she be, waiting to come in and have some dry dog food and get warm in front of the wood stove. We both liked this arrangement.

It soon became clear to me what Flo was doing on these disappearances. One day as I walked out the back door, I found the carcass of a baby goat lying at my feet as a trophy present for me. Uh oh, I thought, some farmer is not going to be very happy with my feral black huntress.

Then Ken died. Flo was with him when he died. The police said they found Ken's boot hidden in a stonewall. They tracked Flo's paw prints and blood from the boot in the snow to the stonewall. I think Flo may have been trying to conceal what he had done.

The day he died, my girlfriends all appeared as if by osmosis to be with me. I was so grief-stricken that I got intense tetany in my fingers from hyperventilating, so my mother had to wipe my nose as my hands clawed up like a chicken foot.

Late in the night, I woke to see a bunch of lumps on my bed in the moonlight. I sat up, disoriented, until I realized all the lumps were my girlfriends sleeping, or passed out, scattered in various positions all around me. I turned to my right, and there was Flo, with her snout on the bed, staring at me quietly with one eyebrow cocked up. She wasn't wagging her tail at all and her eyes were full of concern.

I have to say, Ken's death kicked the shit out of me. As time went by, I didn't get "better"; I seemed to get worse. I knew I was dangling precariously close to insanity. I gave myself permission to be crazy for as long as it took to heal. It ended up that it took one full year of crazy to come out the other side. That was just the way it had to happen. I had to feel it all. I wasn't going to drug away the pain.

I built a hut at the base of The Tree where Ken died. I bent heavy saplings in an arch to create a dome shape and lashed them together until the frame was pretty sturdy. I wove smaller saplings through the frame until it was strong enough to handle the elements. Then I covered this structure with blankets and then with waterproof tarps. I dug a fire pit in the center of the lodge and made a small smoke hole in the roof. I had a heavy Indian blanket covering for the door. The door itself faced East.

I spent as much time as possible in my lodge in the forest. In retrospect, I'm sure my family and friends *did* think this was insane, but they only conveyed to me their love and support. Flo was my constant companion. During this time she only left occasionally to hunt. Most of the time she was by my side. She was probably extremely worried about me too, but we had an amazing time out there. It was an intensely healing time full of sorrow and joy. A magical time.

Even in the dead of winter, we were all right. I had a great sleeping bag that was rated for 40 degrees below zero, and I had Flo, who would curl up next to me on the insulated mat to keep warm. So we were good. The only downside was that the smoke from the fire pit started to seriously hurt my eyes after a while. But by then it was warm weather again so we weren't so dependent on fire for warmth. I began to get better.

On the one-year anniversary of Ken's death, I decided I was going to go to a holy place to learn hands-on energy healing. I wanted to become a healer. The joke was on me, however, because as I began to heal myself, my rebellion gene began to re-emerge. I broke all their stuffy rules, and ultimately got kicked out of the ashram. But I came back home feeling whole and strong and back to my regular naughty self.

I had been gone a month. I walked to the back yard and saw Flo heading home across the back field with a large bird in her mouth. When she saw me she dropped the bird and let out a plaintive howl that made the hair stand up on my neck. I had never heard her howl before. She sounded just like a coyote. I laughed and said, "Well! I guess you really are a coy-dog after all!" She ran frenzied circles around me, yipping like a puppy, delirious in her joy at my return.

"Okay," I said as I hugged her tightly. "I promise I will never leave you again."

As Flo became more socialized, she hunted less and less. Apart from the occasional frog, or the time I found a bloody baby deer skull with tiny antlers, still covered in cartilage and fur, perched proudly in one of my planters—she embraced her domestic dog side. Except for one thing: she *hated* small yappy dogs. Probably the coy-dog instinct was too hard-wired genetically for her to be able to resist killing a small obnoxious creature. I think she couldn't—or wouldn't—distinguish a small domestic dog from a rodent or small game.

The first time it happened (at least while I was present), Flo and I were walking down a remote dirt road in central New Hampshire as an elderly couple walked toward us. They were walking a small, longhaired dog—probably a Pomeranian. When the dog saw Flo it started barking at her in a high-pitched, frantic yip. I felt Flo tense and then silently run at the dog in full kill mode. In a flash, before I could even react, Flo grabbed the dog and shook it like a rag doll, instantly snapping its neck.

The people were screaming, *"Lady! Lady! Lady!"* I was horrified. After many apologies and negotiating and groveling, that little episode cost me $1500.00. Not that this could ever replace a beloved pet, but this was the price they asked for that breed.

Back in the car, I yelled at her, "Jesus Christ, Flo! What the hell am I going to do with you? You just can't kill someone's *pet!* You do that again and you're going to be dog meat. I mean it!"

She looked at me serenely, deliberately obtuse. "What? What are you going on about? I thought that was a groundhog."

More than once, I believe Flo saved my life. When I turned forty, a Mexican shaman woman named Quinn suggested I do a vision quest to celebrate this milestone birthday. She designed it for me. She said I was to do three days in the wilderness with water, but no food, and she allowed me to take a knife, matches for fire—and my dog.

My dog? I said I thought it was pretty unusual for me to be able to take my dog along on a quest that was supposed to be solitary. She agreed that it was—but she said she had seen that my dog was also my spirit guardian and she needed to be there to protect me.

I spent three days deep in the solitary wilderness of coastal Downeast Maine, and it was miserable. At first it was foggy and misty and rainy, as only the Maine coast can be. Then it got humid and the mosquitoes came out in droves. I wondered wryly if the Native Americans of this area, the Penobscot (which means "first light"), had to contend with horrendous mosquitoes on their vision quests. I resorted to rolling "stogies" out of dry oak leaves filled with dry pine needles and "smoking" these cigars, blowing the smoke around my head to keep the mosquitoes away.

On the final night, the mosquitoes were so bad that I dug a body-sized hole in the forest floor with my knife and I buried myself in it. When I woke, it was pitch dark. A light rain had started, and it put out my fire. Then I heard a growl, a low threatening growl very close to my back. All of a sudden Flo attacked whatever it was, and there was a screaming fight between the two animals. They were locked in a ferocious battle to the death. For many minutes, I heard guttural snarls and jaws snapping and screaming and howling—and then nothing.

Dead silence.

Then something started walking slowly toward me where I sat trembling in the dark.

Ho...ly...shit. I braced myself for the worst.

Then Flo rested her snout on my shoulder.

Flo in her later years

Carol Leonard

Flo and I had been together for eight years when I fell in love with Tom Lajoie. Tom was a registered Maine whitewater guide and extreme whitewater kayaker. Flo adored Tom, and she became a great river dog. The outdoor life suited us well. We did a lot of traveling in search of breathtaking rapids for Tom and his paddling friends to run.

One fall, Tom was taking a group of Boston secretaries rafting down the West Branch of the Penobscot River. He was certified to take them down the Exterminator Rapids and the Cribworks, a Class V rapid. It was early October, but there was a definite nip in the air, so I declined to go and instead decided to walk along a small portion of the Appalachian Trail to Nesowadnahunk Falls. Flo and I ambled along in what started out as a rather mild day, but as we walked the temperature seemed to plummet. A cold drizzly rain began to fall. I wasn't really properly dressed for a freezing rain.

I was pretty chilled by the time I got to the falls. I sat down to eat my sandwich. I hadn't seen Flo in a while. I took a bite of my sandwich and then Flo was at my side. She shook her neck and *FWAMP!* the side of my face was covered with orangey brown excrement. My head was dripping in runny human diarrhea. Flo's whole side was covered in human shit where she had rolled in it on the side of the trail, thinking it a lovely perfume.

"Oh my god!" I was gagging. The only thing I could do was dive into the water to get the shit washed off me. I had to pull Flo in the water with me to wash the crap off her, too. On the walk back to my car, I got way *way* too cold. I was drenched and dizzy and disoriented. I could just see the headlines:

"Personal Hygiene Challenged Midwife Succumbs to Hypothermia"

By the time I got to my car, my hands were so frozen that I almost couldn't get the key in the lock. Once in my car, I turned the heat up full blast, but I was still shivering uncontrollably and my teeth were chattering. All I could think about while driving back to the rafting company's guide loft was taking a long, hot shower and putting on my warm, dry clothes. Half way back to the lodge, I heard Flo retching and heaving until she finally vomited partially digested human diarrhea—right into the open woven basket holding my clean clothes.

200

In the lodge's shower facility, the showers were coin operated. I managed to get my quarters in the slot despite my shaking hands. Then I watched in dismay as only a couple of drops dripped out. The showers were on the fritz. At this point, the Boston secretaries returned from their rafting trip, their faces all aglow with excitement.

They were giggling, "Oh my god! Don't you think our guide was so *CUTE!?* What a gorgeous blonde, blue-eyed hunk!"

I stood there glowering at them. Okay, that did it. Be-atches! I stomped off to the bar for some liquid antifreeze—with smelly, disgusting poop in my hair. I guess maybe I should have gone rafting with the secretaries, after all. It certainly would have been more sanitary.

It was when Tom and I and several of his paddling buddies were traveling out West in search of snow-pack-melt rapids that I realized my dog was getting older. Even by conservative guesstimates, Flo was probably somewhere around fifteen years old. The first time I was taken by surprise was when I found her shivering in the night air on a lovely, crisp spring evening. All of a sudden, I realized that she was no longer able to thermo-regulate very well.

I looked at my dog's face closely and saw that, seemingly overnight, her muzzle had become all white. Her black and white coloring reminded me of a nun's habit. Flo had also, as she aged, acquired a serene and saintly demeanor. I took to calling her "Sister Florence Agnes" because if ever there was a Catholic dog, she was it.

Sister Flo fooled a lot of people with that saintly shtick.

On this trip, all the boaters and their dogs hiked several miles into the rugged, dry mountains of Kelly Forks, Idaho. But on the way back, Flo pooped out completely. She refused to move another inch. I was frantic, because it was still quite a way back to our campsite. Stalwart Tom just took it in stride; he acted as if it was no big deal, so as to not embarrass her. He picked Flo up and wrapped her around his neck like a big fur collar and kept walking back to camp. I have a great photo of Tom peeing off the side of the trail with a furry nun wrapped around his shoulders.

When we returned home to NH, Flo had her first seizure. It wasn't so bad, I guess, as seizures go—but it was definitely scary. I brought her to DVM Jim, who did a complete physical, including X-rays.

As we looked at the X-rays, Jim said, "When did she get capped in the ass? See that peppery looking stuff? Her butt is full of buckshot."

I immediately visualized the baby goat carcass, and I knew.

Jim put her on Prednisone. Tom and I adapted to living with a noble senior citizen. We thought she could depart us at any time—but Flo ended up living another astounding *four years.*

She was a huntress up to the very end. In her eighteenth year, I was walking with Sister Florence along our beach in Surry, Maine when we came upon a woman lounging in a beach chair, reading a book. Too late, I saw the two little yappy dogs under her chair. Flo bolted toward her prey, but she was no longer able to outrun me. I flew after her and tackled her just as she got to the chair. I crashed on top of her.

The woman looked from saintly dog to me. I was panting mightily as I crushed my ancient dog. She lowered her sunglasses and said in an acerbic voice, "Over-reacting a bit, aren't we?"

Boy Howdy! For one second, I seriously considered letting Flo loose. But the woman was just another sucker who got conned by Flo's Catholic ruse. At least this time, Flo and I went home without having to shell out any more bribe money.

For several years at the end of her life, Flo went down our road to steal a Milkbone from her friend, Bailey the Bassett Hound. Every single day at the same time. It was about a half-mile trek, and our road was fairly heavy with traffic. Flo always looked both ways when she crossed the road and stayed way over on the shoulder. People called her the "Commuter Dog."

One day, as I was looking out the window, I saw Flo come tottering down the driveway with a stolen Milkbone in her mouth. Directly behind her was a police cruiser with its blue lights flashing. A police officer got out and walked to my door.

He said, "Is this your dog?"

I said, "Why, yes, she is. Is there a problem?"

He said, "Well, I saw her walking down the road and I realized she was, um, elderly. I thought she might need an assist. So I tried to get her to get into my cruiser...but she bit me!" He held out his hand and there was the tiniest nick.

I said sweetly, "I'm terribly sorry about that, but I've always taught her to never accept a ride from a stranger."

He smiled.

I said, "Thank you, Officer, for the police escort. That was very thoughtful."

When Flo was nineteen years of age, I knew the end was getting near. Tom and I had many discussions about the quality of her life and how to determine the end without making her suffer needlessly. In the end, I think I may have kept her here one day longer than I should have—but that one last day was a powerful one.

I was stopped in traffic at a red light, and Flo was in her throne in the back seat. Her window was open. A car pulled up beside us slowly. In my rearview mirror, I saw Flo serenely appraise the people in the next car. Even though her eyes were cloudy, she nodded ever so slightly, like a Queen acknowledging her subjects. Then she turned her head regally to survey her kingdom.

By the time the car came abreast of mine, both the driver and the passenger's faces were wet with tears. They smiled gratefully at the chance to have experienced Flo in her ancient, serene wisdom. It was a split second interaction but I knew, somehow, that it meant the end.

The next morning, as I helped Flo hobble out to pee, I noticed that her urine was filled with pus and blood. She became very anxious, and was agitated all morning.

She cocked her eyebrow up and squared me with her eyes, as if to say, "Really! Carol, you've got to do something. I am *done!*"

She was panting hoarsely. I realized she was in pain. I called Jim and told him that today was the day. He said he would be there in the evening as soon as his office hours were over.

All day, Flo was anxious and looked frightened. She knew. Finally, I started chanting to her. I sang repeatedly:

> The river she is flowing…Flowing and growing.
> The river, she is flowing…Down to the sea.
> Mother carry me…Your dog I will always be.
> Mother carry me…Down to the sea.

This seemed to soothe and comfort her tremendously. I must've sung it to her a hundred times. Oh, I loved this dog so much. My protector. My best friend. I so didn't want to see her in pain like this. Please, Jim…hurry.

I said to her, "I know you think I'm a knucklehead and that you need to protect me. But I'll be okay…honest. You can go now. You've done a terrific job. I will see you on the Otherside."

My dear friend, Kudra, came to be with us that evening for the crossing over. We sat quietly talking and waiting, with Flo lying between us on the couch. Flo seemed more at ease then. Jim arrived and I told him that we were ready. Jim crouched down in front of us and shaved a small area on Flo's leg. Then he injected his lethal potion. Tom, Kudra and I had our hands on Flo as we felt her breathing still. Her head was in my lap and she closed her eyes…and she was gone.

With tears streaming down our faces, we wrapped her in some rich brocade fabric I had, and we made a beautiful shroud by wrapping brightly colored ribbons around and around her. I adorned her with some antique Celtic silver jewelry. Kudra lit a nine-day candle. Tom dug a grave next to Ken's memorial bench. We placed Flo gently in the ground—her snout facing East. I sat by her grave for a long time.

Godspeed, my good friend. May your spirit fly with the Great Canine Spirit.

That was a long time ago. I've had other dogs since. I used to dream about her all the time after she died. Now she appears in my dreams only rarely. But, always when I wake after a dream about Flo, I have tears of joy and my heart is full. I know she remembers me. My Spirit Dog. She is waiting for me. She is waiting on the Otherside.

Nice Rack!

This is a picture of a REAL MOOSE (left) checking out our fake moose (right) in the field at Bad Beaver on 11/25/16. The fake moose is my "birthday moose" that Tom cut out of 500 lbs. of steel with an acetylene torch. It has been in the field for several years.

It looks like the cow is saying, "Hmm…the strong silent type, eh?"

(Photo by neighbor Ryan Hartley)

WINTER

WINTER

A SCREAM IN THE NIGHT

I just heard a "vixen scream", the sound of foxes mating outside my bedroom window. I am amazed, because even after a half century of knowing what this sound is, it still makes the hair on the back of my neck stand up and makes me hyper-alert. Now I know that when I hear that bloodcurdling scream, the mating foxes are locked in a backwards "copulatory knot" which can last for over two hours. God, I would be screaming too.

But now this haunting sound makes me smile as I remember the first time I ever heard it. I was a twelve-year-old, prepubescent girl and for some reason I had fallen asleep on the padded window seat in my family's sun porch instead of my bedroom. It was the middle of the night and the jalousie windows of the sun porch were open. I sat bolt upright as I heard the unmistakable sound of a woman screaming in intense pain. My heart was beating like a drum and I felt a little nauseous. Then I heard it again! It definitely was a woman in terrible trouble—maybe even being strangled.

I could barely breathe, but I slipped on my sneakers and slid out of the side door of the sun porch, and ran across the lawn, then through the long field toward the sound. It was very dark but there was enough of a slight new moon to make landmarks eerily identifiable. It sounded like it was coming from the little pond that I had named "Cherry Pond" for the first spring blossoms of the wild cherry trees surrounding the water. I had no idea, obviously, what I would do exactly when I found the source of the terror—I just knew I had to help this struggling woman.

When I got to Cherry Pond, the screaming stopped. I sat quietly with my heart pounding in my ears and waited, shaking uncontrollably. When I heard it again, it was so close by that I also heard a soft "whooping" sound accompanying the terrible scream. Ah, so it was animals. With tremendous relief, I lay back on my back in the tall dry grass and stilled my heart and listened with wonder at the horrific, primal sounds. I had not a clue as to what was going on—but the emergent nature of it all had dissipated. The tension drained out of my lips and fingertips. I watched the clouds scudding quickly across the small crescent of the moon, a "fingernail moon" as my mother called it. Eventually, the screams stopped and I didn't hear them again.

The next day, my mother was unloading our fabulous new 1960's avocado-colored dishwasher. I told her about the screaming and about going to investigate in the dark. She was accustomed to her oldest and most feral child running around in the woods and streams unfettered.

She said, "Carol, did it ever occur to you to be afraid?"

I answered honestly, "No, actually, I thought it was pretty cool sounding."

She stopped what she was doing and gave me what my siblings and I called "The Look." Then she sighed and continued putting dishes away.

Now as I lie in my bed, I am in wonderment at where my life has led me since that night. Little did I know then that my entire *life* would be enmeshed in the primal sounds of women, of women crying out in the night in their agony and their ecstasy as they brought forth new life. New life…as, in due time, the mother vixen would soon be licking the blood and the fluid off her newborn kit. New life…and that there would be a thousand women and a thousand times I watched the moon as they cried in fear and in joy as their bodies and souls made that sacred journey. New life…and that I would be so honored to witness this miracle over and over again.

I believe my path was preordained in the moon on the night that a brave young girl ran *toward* the scream.

SEEING GOD

In the summer of my eighteenth year, so that would be 1968, and beyond any reasonable human decision making process, I decided to do a solo peyote trip in the woods near my family's home in Bedford, New Hampshire. Why I thought I could just cruise through that experience without guidance is still beyond me—but, hey, I was just a feral kid, Mother Nature's chosen child.

My girlfriend, Nancy, had a '53 Chevy that had formerly been a Checker cab, a huge boat of an automobile that she named "Glide." She had driven back to NH from southwest Texas with a bushel of peyote buttons in the trunk that she had picked with some sketchy hitchhiker. She dropped off a few buttons for me and then continued on to Canada in search of more misadventures, I guess.

I decided to ingest my peyote on top of of a steep, rocky hill behind our house that we called "Indian Tower." On top of that hill there were huge bushes of mountain laurel and scratchy junipers and a tall tower of piled up rocks that looked very ancient. Ever since my younger siblings and I were kids, we had created a legend that it was built by peoples native to our land as a sacred ceremonial site. In retrospect, it was probably built by some farmer, or even the Boy Scouts; but I loved that place with all my heart and spent a lot of time there growing up.

I can't really remember the specifics of how I actually got the peyote to stay down. I do remember it tasted like earwax and made me gag, so I mashed it and mixed it with coca-cola and struggled to gulp it down, fighting my gag reflex the whole time. Somehow I knew to avoid the fine hairs inside the button as those contained strychnine. But I did it, I got it down. One button? Two buttons? I don't remember, but whatever it was... it was way too much.

I was lying on the rocks basking in the sun when the first wave of anxiety washed over me. Uh-oh. This didn't feel right at all. I became very disoriented. My heart started racing. My lips and fingertips got numb. I got impossibly hot and started sweating profusely. I was panting. I had just enough time to flip over on my stomach before the vomiting began. Huge gallon buckets of green slime ejected from my heaving body. Oh my god. What had I done? How stupid was this? I had just wanted to "be one with Nature" and now I was pretty sure I'd poisoned myself.

And then an evilness crept into me...terrifying me. Something wrong and strong and awful and I was never going to escape it. I had to fight. Shaking. Crying. Overwhelmed by fear, I pissed myself. I fought and fought and fought for I don't know how long, my breath coming in huge gasps of terror, an inescapable, powerful grip, strangling me with panic. I couldn't walk. I could barely crawl. Was I going to die? Then a sadness came with tears streaming down my face. Shaking. Exhausted. I blacked out. I don't know for how long. Then I saw a squint of sunlight.

When I opened my eyes and raised my head, I saw I was still lying at the base of Indian Tower. Fortunately the debilitating nausea was gone. I actually felt a *lot* better, although I could tell by my impaired vision that I was still incredibly high. I tentatively tried sitting up. I got my bearings a little bit. Not so bad. I believed I had survived some kind of brutal initiation from Hell. I was sitting quietly, consciously regulating my breathing, when silently a beautiful Monarch butterfly landed on my hand. She was poised on my knuckle, methodically washing her antennae with her front legs and mouth parts, bending first one antenna, then the other. I swear she looked right up at me, nonchalant, and then fanned her gorgeous orange wings up and down as if to dry them.

I felt a burst of joy and awe at the beauty of this simple gift from Nature. Tears sprang to my eyes. This world is so complex and extraordinary and breathtaking! But..when I looked out over my fanning new friend to the forest beyond...I realized everything was *orange*. EVERYTHING. I lived in a surreal orange landscape for the rest of the trip. I adapted but it did serve to illustrate to me how crazy messed up I still was.

Then I noticed that the surrounding forest was shining before me. The leaves on the trees were emitting light and the trunks of the trees were luminous. The dappled forest burst into bird song, almost as if to the music of the spheres. I saw more shades and nuances of color than I had ever seen before, although my eyes were still seeing as through an orange filter. My sensory gating was thrown wide open. I felt synchronized with everything around me. The feeling of unity with all of creation was pure bliss. I was one with all sentient beings, the trees and the plants and the birds and the insects, merging with the surrounding environment, exploding into the universe. Each bird was aware of my state and watched and cared for me deeply.

I was pure energy, one with all being, at peace with all that could be perceived. Being permeated all. And I knew in that moment that the Cosmos wasn't created out of chaos but out of LOVE. A love for all that ever was, a love for all that is now and a love for all that will ever be. I was bursting with love from the stars in all the still exploding heavens.

And this love was God.

A CHRISTMAS STORY

This is a story about my son, Milan, at Christmastime when he was about six years old. But before I begin this story, I want to say that his name is pronounced *MY-lan*…it's an old Celtic family name, it was my great-great-grandfather's name. Milan Leonard was a Maine Yankee and I have his honorable discharge papers from the Civil War.

So, when Milan was about six years old, we were doing last minute Christmas shopping at Zayre's in Concord. When we came out of the store, a homeless man named Norman was standing, as usual, slumped over his shopping cart, silent. Canned Christmas carols were merrily blasting from a loudspeaker somewhere in front of the store. As we walked past Norman to our car, Milan stared hard at him.

I have to explain that Norman was a "fixture" in Concord in the early 1980s. He was a small, swarthy man with greasy dark hair, whose pants were way too big for him; and even though he wore suspenders, the bare top of his hairy butt-crack was always visible. (This look is totally in style these days.) All of Norman's possessions were in his shopping cart. He also always had a baseball bat at the ready in his cart…and I'm sure it wasn't because he was an avid ball player. There were rumors that he had killed someone.

When we got in the car, Milan was looking straight ahead. He was very quiet. I said, "What's on your mind, Mi?"

He said, "Does Norman have any family that's going to come be with him for Christmas? Is he going to be alone for Christmas?"

"I don't know. Probably."

"How can that happen? How can that be?"

I took a deep breath. "OK, let's talk about poverty and homelessness."

I tried to outline for him as best I could the probable reality of Norman's life.

Driving home, I glanced over and Milan's face was awash in tears. I realized that this was the first time that my son was really painfully, brutally aware of the disparities and cruelties of our culture.

When we got home, he went upstairs and threw himself on his bed, sobbing as though his heart was breaking. This was horrible. My poor child.

I grabbed a box of Kleenex and sat on the side of his bed. I wiped his tears. He blew his nose. He said, "It's just so sad, Mom."

"I know. What can we do to make this better?"

He was quiet for a moment. "I know. Let's make him some cookies… but not Christmas cookies, because that might bum him out."

"Great idea. How about chocolate chip?"

After the cookies were made and in a tin, Milan was quiet again. He said, "It's not enough."

I thought, "Oh dear God, please don't ask to invite Norman to our house for Christmas."

He said, "Let's also get a gift certificate from McDonald's for some Happy Meals."

"Perfect."

When we got the gift certificate and added it to the tin, we drove to Zayre's but Norman was nowhere to be seen. I drove to all the spots where the homeless usually congregated—along the railroad tracks and along the Merrimack River—but we didn't find him. I said, "Honey, we'll take one last pass by Zayre's but if he's not there, we've got to give it up."

But when we went back to Zayre's, there Norman was, slumped over his shopping cart as usual. We pulled up along the sidewalk. I said to Milan, "Ready?"

"Ready."

We got out of the car and walked up to Norman. Milan handed the cookie tin towards him. He said, "We made some cookies for you."

Norman looked angry, although he *always* looked angry. I thought, "Oh dear God, please don't swear at my kid."

Instead, Norman grabbed a pack of cigarettes from his shirt pocket and handed them to Milan. He said, "Here, take these, kid."

Milan hesitated and looked up at me, questioning. I stepped in between them. "Thanks, Norman...but he's trying to quit." Then I said under my breath, "Take the cookies, Norman."

Norman took the cookies and went back and slumped over his cart.

When we got back in the car, Milan was looking straight ahead. He said, "What just happened?"

I sighed. "OK, now let's talk about pride…"

BROKE DOWN IN DOG POOP ALLEY

The infamous Dog Poop Alley

Tom is helping me pack. We are rushing around in the pre-dawn dark throwing stuff in my rucksack. He brings up his crampons from the basement and an old Nalgene water bottle that he blows some dead spiders out of. I am stuffing layers and layers of clothing to bring with me, extra pair of dry socks, extra dry glove liners. The weather report says it is going to be very windy—below zero with the wind chill factor. I add Tom's wind proof balaclava.

Tom is grinning at me. He used to teach the R.O.P.E. course for Concord High students, and they did a "winter survival" weekend. I think he is getting a huge amount of amusement now that his wife is heading out to be one with the frigid elements.

He says, "Knock 'em dead, honey."

"Wise ass," I say as I peck him on the cheek and head for my car.

I have signed up for the *"Becoming an Outdoors Woman"* winter survival course sponsored by the New Hampshire Fish and Game Department. Really, if I want to be a serious nature blogger, I figure I need to have a little more experience with adverse conditions out in the field. I am a little nervous attempting something new at this advanced age, but I am also excited.

Half way to the course, a winter squall blows in and creates severe whiteout conditions. I put my Jeep in 4-wheel drive. Another Jeep from Massachusetts is tailgating me. I can't go any faster because there is a little dark car in front of me…besides, the road is way too shitty to drive any faster. I gently tap my brakes to signal, "get off my ass, buddy" to the Mass. car. He sticks to me like aggressive glue.

Suddenly, the little black car in front of me slams on its brakes. The road is sheer ice! I swear and slam on my brakes to avoid rear-ending the little black car, and I swerve sideways. Then I see a red Camry in front of the little black car skid sideways, hit the snow bank, and flip straight up in the air, and then come crashing down on its roof on the other side of the snow bank. *Holy shit!*

The little black car and I pull over immediately. The Mass Jeep leans on its horn angrily as it speeds by.

"Massholes!" I yell at them as they disappear down the highway.

Four black haired, olive skinned boys, probably in their early twenties, leap out and rush to the upside-down driver's side of the car. They start digging in the snow with their hands like dogs dig for a bone. Frantically, they are digging…digging…digging, scooping and sending the snow flying backwards behind them. I am standing on the snow bank watching this. I am assuming, with the way the roof of the car is flattened like a pancake, that the driver has not survived the crash. One of the boys has called 911.

The boys have dug down to the driver's side window, which is shattered. I see movement! A man's face is at the window—a very *pale* face.

I kneel down, "Sir, are you alone in your car?"

He answers weakly, "Yes."

I see his glasses, and I reach in and get them before they get lost. The man sticks his head out of the window. He is blinking and looking around. He looks like Punxsutawney Phil crawling out of his hole. I am hoping he doesn't see his shadow. For some bizarre reason, when the man crawls out of his window—a bunch of cereal boxes come out with him.

The man sits in the snow beside his car, still blinking, looking very dazed and shocked. Other than a few small cuts on his forehead, he seems to be in perfect health. He has been saved by the snow—and the boys. I sit with him until a first responder arrives. A small Jeep with flashing lights pulls up and a uniformed man who looks exactly like Eric Estrada in CHIPS steps out. I figure that my groundhog friend is in good hands now.

I touch the man gently on the shoulder as I leave. "Dude, you are the luckiest man on the planet right now."

I approach the four gorgeous boys who are now standing quietly to the side. I shake their hands. I say, "You guys did a great job. You saved that man's life. Thank you for all you've done." I notice one of the boys has tears on his cheek.

I drive like a snail the rest of the way to the hunting lodge.

At the hunting lodge, it is sheer bedlam. There are women of all ages and shapes and sizes—all excited and yelling to old friends and laughing and screeching. The noise is deafening. It sounds like about 1000 migratory birds that have all landed in the same tree. There are 70 wild women in all. The male Conservation Officers who will be teaching some of the courses are huddled against the walls, eyes bulging in disbelief at the racket. They look like they are overwhelmed by the enormous amount of unopposed estrogen whirling around the room.

I watch as the women who have signed up for the "Shoe & Shoot" course march off with their rifles hoisted over their shoulders. Macho girls. They make me smile because they remind me of Elmer Fudd. "W-w-where is that cwazy wabbit?"

Brad, the Conservation Officer who is teaching our course, is an ex-military search & rescue guy who first goes over all the necessary gear to avoid frostbite and hypothermia—with resulting amputation and death, respectively. We have two assignments today. One is to learn how to dig a snow cave for shelter if we are trapped above tree line (probably not in my future) and the other is how to build a lean-to shelter out of natural materials from the woods (probably happening in the foreseeable future.) We are to construct the shelter, build a fire, get water from the creek, and boil water over the fire to make hot cocoa.

The snow caves are dug into enormous snow mounds from the plow around the perimeter of the parking lot. Digging the cave reminds me of being a kid when we used to get *huge* amounts of snow in NH and we would dig forts in the drifts. The plowed snow is hard and the digging pretty much sucks. Chinking away with a shovel and an ice pick, I'm totally planning to *never* be caught above tree line and have to do this.

When the cave is done, we are to crawl in to see how it fits, how it feels. I lie there for a total of about 10 seconds before my claustrophobia kicks into high gear. My heart starts crashing, I get sweaty, I'm finding it hard to breath. *MIDWIFE FOUND BURIED ALIVE!*

I dive back out through the entrance and look up at my co-survivors. "I'd rather die," I say.

The one thing that I learn in this course that is absolutely worth the price of admission is a nifty fire-starting secret. I think this is the nuts! You can make your own homemade "prepared tinder" for igniting kindling in wind and rain and holocausts by liberally coating cotton balls with Vaseline. *Vaseline!* Store the greased-up cotton balls in a Ziploc bag in your rucksack until you need a rip-roaring fire to survive the elements. The petroleum jelly in the Vaseline burns fiercely—long enough to get the kindling blazing. I have a blast running around like a fledgling arsonist, starting everyone's fires with these ingenious slimy cotton balls.

For lunch, we have caribou, venison and bear stew, and it is delicious. Over stew, I am regaling my lunch-table mates with the story of how Tom and I met. They are laughing hysterically but sometimes I wonder what they are really thinking. Cougar…certainly. Pedophile? Quite possibly.

After lunch, the little hemlock and spruce lean-to shelter my group makes is cozy and cunnin' (actually, somehow I wander in with the wrong group—but this is okay—they let me survive with them anyway). The fire pit has a wind-wall made of snow that also reflects the heat back into the lean-to. There is one woman who is about 6 feet tall and is an Amazonian Goddess of the Fire. She is cutting down whole trees with a little ax. She is chopping like a mad woman, working herself up into a sweat, chopping with determination and machine-like precision. I'm thinking if I ever get lost in the woods—I want to get lost with *her*.

In no time at all, the Fire Goddess has a bonfire raging that is big enough to burn a few witches on. We rig up a stand with rocks for the pot of water to boil on. The Fire Goddess whittles some handles from sticks to lift the pot up without danger. By mid-afternoon, the first round of hot cocoa goes around and everyone is surviving. I decline the cocoa, wishing for a Margarita. Different survival mechanisms, I guess.

When the day is over and we are back in the hunting lodge, I am definitely feeling like a Winter Warrioress. I feel like I am walking a little taller, a little prouder. This was fun. I will definitely do another *BOW* course in the future.

Maybe by then I'll have the ovaries enough to do the "Shoe & Shoot" biathlon course.

Back at home, later that night, I wake from dozing in front of the wood stove where I have been attempting to read *"Ten Essentials for Your Survival Pack."* Tom has gone to bed. I realize that our old dog, Gladys, has not come in yet. This can mean only one thing—she's out having a midnight snack at the compost pile. This also means, because she is a geriatric dog, that she will be shitting in the upstairs hall tonight. Dammit! Cussed dog.

I go stomping out the path that Tom has snowblowed for our dogs, called "Poop Alley." I am yelling to her, but I know it is useless, as Gladys is stone deaf. The compost pile is in our back field. The path is pretty dark and it is sheer ice, but I know my way by heart so I am marching along, in broken clogs, at a pretty good clip. What I don't know is that there is a big bough fallen across the path, and I collide with it full-tilt. I skid on the ice sideways, hit the snow bank and flip straight up in the air, and then come crashing down on my left side. I hear something snap but maybe it was just the tree branch.

"Help!"

"HELP!"

"***HELP!*** I think I broke my arm!"

I am lying in Dog Poop Alley yelling my bloody head off. I look up to the sky in agony. The stars are wheeling brightly overhead and I feel nauseous. I realize no one can hear me yelling—certainly not Gladys, as if she cares. Only now do I realize that I forgot my Vaseline soaked cotton balls that I could light and use for rescue flares.

And wasn't it only just a few hours ago that I was a proud Winter Warrioress? Now I am lying, crippled, in frozen dog shit. Gladys comes sauntering back down the path and sniffs me, like, "Um, dude, what are you doing lying on the ground?"

The smell of Gladys's compost-breath is so hellacious that I get up immediately. I snivel and gimp my way back to the house. I crawl into bed and tell Tom what happened. He says I need to get my arm x-rayed.

I sigh. Who ever heard of a Winter Warrioress with a frickin' *cast* on?

POSTSCRIPT: The x-ray shows that this Winter Weenie does indeed have a radial head fracture of the elbow, the classic ice-fall break for old ladies, which means a cast for 4 to 6 weeks. Feeling *very* sorry for myself at the present moment. *WAH!*

THE BONE DOCTORS

Chucky, the evil troll

I am rushing to my appointment at [unnamed/incompetent] Orthopedics when I knock over one of those horrible little porcelain figurines that come in the Red Rose tea boxes. I have knocked it off the front desk at work; the woman at the front desk collects them. It is the one I hate the most, a creepy little trolly guy with outstretched arms. Secretly, I call him "Chucky."

Lydia, the woman at the front desk at the health center today, leans over and picks up a tiny little arm from the floor.

"You broke his arm off," she accuses me.

"Which arm?" I ask, my suspicions rising. I already know.

"His left one." Her eyes dart involuntarily to my left arm that she believes is now acting as a war-club on a mission to wipe out all her scary trolls.

I have taken out creepy little Chucky with my left arm, which now is sheathed in fiberglass and about 17 pounds of ace bandages, the splint that the soft-spoken PA at Emergent Care put on my broken arm nine days ago. The arm that is supposed to be re-cast in a permanent cast today.

I have an uneasy feeling of foreboding.

"This is weird. I wonder what *this* is all about," Lydia says as she tries to re-attach Chucky's arm.

"I know what it means. It's a premonition of things to come."

Lydia looks at me like now it's confirmed that I'm nuts.

"No, really," I continue, "I don't want a new cast today. I *love* this splint. It's comfortable and yummy and I can still work with it on. I don't have a twinge of pain. As my grandfather always said, 'If it ain't broke—don't fix it.' Oh…wait…"

I head out the door.

I am supposed to see the Orthopedic Specialist, but I never do see him. I wouldn't be able to pick him out of a line-up if my life depended on it. Instead, I see his PA, a perky young woman in her mid-thirties (although at my age, all these doctors are starting to look like they are twelve). She is very self-confident and personable. She removes my beloved splint, pokes around for a minute, and then sends me to Radiology—yet again. I'm going to start glowing in the dark.

I sit alone in Radiology for an hour. My left arm lies limply in my lap.

I am very protective of it. My arm is like a hermit crab—it is exposed and flaccid and vulnerable to predation. It doesn't like being out of its shell.

I am trying to read a magazine one-handed without much success. Have you ever tried reading a magazine with one hand? Try it—it sucks. The magazine keeps flopping over to one side. I give up and just stare at the dusty plastic plant in front of me.

Finally someone comes in the room and asks if I'm from "Ortho." I nod "Yes." She says no one told them I was there. Effing fabulous.

The x-ray room is surreal in a dim subterranean half-light, with two enormous older women shuffling around, their white scrubs glowing with an otherworldly gloom. The woman with the backside that is two ax-handles wide, tosses me a lead apron to tie around my middle. I struggle to tie it with one hand. I give up and sit down. There is not one possibility in hell that I could be pregnant.

All of a sudden I get a deja vu of working in Moscow. I am back working as a midwife in Radom #23, the maternity hospital in Moscow in 1990—when it was still the Soviet Union. The only thing that's different is that no one is smoking cigarettes and stubbing the butts out on the floor.

The woman instructs me to straighten my arm out across the table and then twist my elbow 90 degrees. I look up at her, my mouth dropped open. She's kidding me, right? She repeats her instruction.

I say, as politely as I can muster, "Ma'am, if I could do that little maneuver—I wouldn't be here."

The woman roughly grabs my wrist and wrenches my arm out-straight across the table and then presses it down. I see stars. Seriously, I feel like I am going to pass out.

I amend my deja vu. Even the ***orderlies*** in Moscow were more warm and fuzzy than these women.

I mutter, "Dosvidaniya!" in Russkie under my breath as I leave.

Back with the hipster PA, I look at the radial head of my elbow on the x-rays. The fracture is clearly visible. It is "displaced" and "stepped-down" as she shows me with a pointer. She states that there is a possibility that I may need to have a pin put in my elbow. I wince. This was not on my screen *at all*.

Here's where I believe I made the fateful mistake that changed the course of everything.

"I don't have any insurance," I say, "Well, I do, but it's 'catastrophic.' I'll be paying for all this out-of-pocket."

Did her demeanor just change subtly—or am I just being paranoid?

"Oh, well, in that case, let's just re-splint your arm and check it again in two weeks." With this she steps out of the door.

The door opens again and a young bebopper woman with a blonde ponytail steps in. She is chewing gum.

"Hi, I'm Andrea," she grins. "I'll be doing your splint today."

I peer at her nametag. It has large blue letters after her name. **CMA**. Certified Medical Assistant.

She pulls out a roll of the splint material that hardens into fiberglass. She fumbles with the closure on the package.

She says, "I may need your help holding this while it hardens."

I ask, "Do you do a lot of these?"

"No, never," she giggles.

The CMA has me twist my left hand away from my body and pinch the cast material with my fingers to hold it in place while it hardens.

I swear I hear Chucky's evil laugh over the intercom.

Later, I leave work early because I just don't feel "right." The top of my forearm has a dull ache. I tell Tom that I feel like shit and that I'm going to skip dinner and just go to bed.

I wake at 2:00 AM and know that something is really, *really wrong*. My arm is screaming, the pain is unbearable. I immediately run to the bathroom and vomit. I tell Tom something is really wrong with the cast— it's making me sick. Tom gently unwraps the splint and removes the fiberglass. He thinks it's too tall, too far up under my armpit, and maybe was suppressing my brachial artery. This may have been what made me feel so nauseous.

I can hear Tom downstairs sawing off the top of the cast with his sawsall. What a guy—what a sweetie—up in the middle of the night sawing off the Iron Maiden to free the old lady. He comes back upstairs and rewraps it. I take 800 mg. of Ibuprofen and try to sleep.

Two hours later I am moaning and writhing in pain. This is worse than natural childbirth! I run and vomit again. I can't do this. I tell Tom to take it off again—I'll just keep it off until I can be re-splinted at Emergent Care.

I lie with my poor arm draped, useless and throbbing, across my torso. The pain is excruciating. I realize my arm has just been re-broken.

In the morning light we see the culprit. The fiberglass splint is twisted like a spiral pasta. The shape of the cast had been forcing my radius in an abnormal rotation, stressing and re-breaking the fracture. The past ten days of healing have been negated and I have been set back to Day One. I am distraught.

Don't ever say Chucky didn't try to warn me.

POSTSCRIPT: Contrary to medical advice, I never did put my cast back on. I signed up for a strength training class for senior women. I worked out *gently* with 80+-year-old women, doing weights and resistance training with bungee cords with those lovely ladies until I was able to pick my nose with my left hand. My arm was completely healed in less than six weeks thanks to those feisty old gals. (And now I wear YakTraks to get old deaf Gladys out of the compost pile at night.) This getting old is not for the faint of heart.

My Bloody Valentine

Carol in the vixen's lair

I open my eyes and realize it's Valentine's Day! I am excited because I get to spend the whole day with Tom, as he's taken the day off from his compulsive work schedule to appease me. I roll over and pinch him. He squints open one sleepy blue eye.

I say, "Happy V.D. Tom!"

He yawns and stretches. "So what do you want to do today?"

I say, "What I really want to do for Valentine's Day is to look for fox blood in the snow."

Tom rolls his eyes up and looks at the ceiling. He stares for many minutes before he sighs, "Some people really know how to party."

Probably not the sexiest thing he had in mind.

I learned the day before, when I did a winter mammal-tracking afternoon with a naturalist for the NH Forest Society, that in mid-February fox pair up as mating season begins. The female fox territorially marks the snow with her blood as she enters estrus, announcing that she is fertile. I have never seen this before.

Tom gets up and begins to dress. "I'm pretty sure I know of a place where we will see this." What a good sport. I quickly pack a picnic lunch.

Tom grew up in this countryside and when he was a kid, he and his brothers, the Lajoie boys, used to roam the woods far and wide. We drive to the hills that surround the water reservoir for the City of Concord. We park in front of a sign that says:

NO TRESPASSING. PUBLIC WATER SUPPLY.

We start hiking up a walking trail, our boots crunching in the snow. Our two black mutt-girls, Gladys and Phaedra, are running around insanely happy to be in the wild, sniffing every little piece of scat they can find, and then peeing on it. It really is so good to be out in the woods.

After several minutes, the trail opens out on to a wide frozen beaver pond surrounded by snow-covered hills. I whisper, "Wow. I never knew this was here. This is beautiful."

Tom grins, "Yeah, I used to fish this pond when I was a kid."

We walk around the perimeter of the pond checking out animal tracks. Snowshoe hares, fishers, coyotes—although it is increasingly harder to distinguish the coyote prints from our domestic dogs who are still bounding around looking delirious with their tongues hanging out and their eyes bulging with excitement. We find several moss-covered porcupine dens in the banks along the edge of the pond, the entrances filled with porcupine poop and tons of quills that have rubbed off as the porkies go in and out.

We head off the pond and scramble up a ravine and up a hill that has the remains of an old fire tower at the summit. It is pretty steep going, and half way up the hill I feel like I just might keel over and die. I am gasping for air. Tom is bounding up ahead with the dogs, although in my defense, even the dogs have slowed down a little bit. They keep looking back at me as I haul my pathetic 60+-year-old butt up the trail. Gawd. I have *got to* start exercising.

Tom waits for me near the top as I huff and puff up to him, my face beet red. He looks down the hill and says, with a trace of nostalgia in his voice, "My brother, Ken, and I used to ride our mountain bikes up this hill when we were in our twenties."

I look at him. Is he kidding? That was, like what, last year for him? Jaysus, what a weisenheimer.

We go over the top of the hill facing the north side where we get a clear view of Long Pond, the water reservoir, through the winter barren trees. The sky is overcast, leaden with coming snow. We find a great dry log and kick the snow in front of it in a circle to make a little fire to cook our hot dogs for lunch. I don't usually make a habit of eating nitrite-laden tube-steaks, but for some reason, there is nothing better in the whole world than a hot dog burnt to splitting over an open fire—with a little Grey Poupon mustard.

Getting the fire going with snow-damp leaves and miscellaneous wood takes a little patience, but Tom gets a rip-roaring, spark-crackling fire going soon enough. It gets cozy and warm. We sit together on the log with our hot dog sticks stuck in the coals, listening to the wiener fat start to make the coals sizzle. We place two tube-steaks on mustard-covered bread and we share a bottle of Chardonnay. (I know, I know—hot dogs with Pouilly Fuisse—or "Fussy Pussy" as Tom calls it. Yeesh, how tacky.)

I look at my husband. I am filled with such fondness for him.

I toast him, "Tom, it doesn't get much better than this. Happy Lupercalia!"

He grins at me, "There is nothing else in the world I'd rather be doing right now. This sure beats being home on the couch watching the Daytona 500."

At this moment, for some reason, Gladys and Phaedra get into a horrible fight over a prize stick. This hasn't happened in *years*. Why this stick is so important is beyond us, but they are seriously locked in a death grip. Both dogs were happily chewing at each end of a long stick, an arrangement that was fine until they got to the middle of the stick—then bedlam ensued. Neither one will back down. The racket is deafening. It looks potentially physically damaging. The only thing I can think of to do to break them up is to stand up and klonk each dog on the head with the empty wine bottle. This gets their attention. They remove their teeth from each other's throats.

Tom just looks at me. He says, "Honey, that's the most redneck thing I have ever seen in my life." (Coming from him—that's something.)

When we are done our Valentine's snack, we trample out the fire with the snow and pack up to leave. Tom walks over the hill and I go to pee behind a pine tree. Peeing in the snow is a feat in itself, and the only sage advice I have for women in the winter is to be sure that you are not inadvertently squatting over the back of your parka. Otherwise, you will be soggy and will have to pretend all the way home that you spilled wine on your coat. (I speak from experience here.)

I follow Tom's tracks to where he is standing looking out over a cliff. He turns to me and his eyes are sparkling. He points down to the huge granite out-cropping below and there they are. Woven in and out of the myriad caves is a network of bloody trails in the snow. Vixen blood!

I am speechless. I feel so honored and grateful to be able to witness this. I guess only a midwife would think that stumbling upon estrus blood in the wild is the coolest thing she has ever seen. Looking at all the blood, if I hadn't known in advance what was going on; I would have assumed it was carnage from the bloody demise of many hapless little varmints.

This grisly scene makes me want to know more. Later I research *"Estrus in Vulpes vulpes."* Here's what I find: Estrus refers to the phase when the female fox is sexually receptive ('in heat'.) The vixen exhibits a sexually receptive behavior, a situation that may be signaled by visible physiologic changes. Proestrus, judged by vulval swelling and reddening, begins 7 days before estrus and is accompanied by sanguineous (bloody) discharge. A signal trait of estrus is the *lordosis reflex*, in which the vixen spontaneously elevates her hindquarters. A single mating, followed by an extremely long "copulatory lock," can average 1 hour 58 minutes."

OWWW! No wonder foxes scream so loud and so long in the night.

Satisfied that we have found what we were looking for, we slide and sidestep our way down the steep, snow covered incline back to our truck. Such an awe-inspiring, wonderful day. I so appreciate Tom for being such an understanding guy.

Guess it's time to go home and practice my lordosis reflex.

MEDUSA

Carol feeding a Canada Jay

I call my snowmobile Medusa. I named her that because she is black with yellow flames shooting out of her hood and along her sides. The flames remind me of snakes writhing from the Gorgon's head. Medusa is fearless and powerful—and patient.

Right now I am listening to Medusa's throaty rumble as I get up the courage to follow in AJ's tracks. His tracks have gone up a steep incline, a cliff face actually, and have disappeared over the top. I look back at Tom who nods encouragement with his dark helmet. Tom is traveling behind me in case I get stuck—or worse. We are bushwhacking up an uncharted mountainside to an underground cave high above. What if I flip over with Medusa's 1000 pounds landing on top of me? Then what? In the middle of nowhere with no cell phone coverage, crushed, unable to breathe, no chance of being airlifted out.

Oh, for godsake, Carol, get a grip.

I gauge the incline ahead, which looks to me to be at least an 80-degree angle. I look out over the vista behind me and get a little vertigo. Below me is a breathtaking vista of lakes dotted with islands and white-capped mountains as far as the eye can see. *Rumble.* I can feel Medusa's impatience and give her permission to go. She bounds up the mountainside like it is a mere speed bump, not a hint of a skid.

I love this sled. She has such good gription.

In my youth, I was a purist and scoffed at snow machines. Give me a good set of snowshoes or cross-country skis any day. No motorized snow sports for me! But several years ago, in my late fifties, Tom gave me a Polaris Indy 500 for a present. She has heated hand-warmers, heated face-shield, a comfy stretch-out seat, reverse. Actually, she is the nuts. Her speedometer says she can go 120 MPH. Yeah, right. I have never even gone close to *half* that speed.

I realize now I would never have seen so many natural wonders right in our own backyard in NH and Maine if it wasn't for two-stroke smoke. Like today, as we traverse up the side of Tucker Mountain in the remainder of the early spring snow. We are looking for an underground cave towards the summit that AJ knows about.

We stop for lunch at a sunny spot on the slope and unpack our sandwiches and Genesee beer. I have already floundered in the snow up to my crotch and had to roll over on my back to get my legs free, so now I sit on Medusa's strong, warm seat munching my sandwich where I am safe from getting swallowed up by quick-snow.

AJ says in wonderment, "How is it that these guys always find us?"

He holds up a piece of bread in his hands as a silent shadow swoops from a branch and snatches the bread from his fingers. A Canada jay— *Perisoreus canadensis*—also nicknamed the "Camp Robber." This little guy is about 10-13 inches long and is slightly larger than a robin. He is gray on his upper body and white on the lower part, and has a white forehead and throat and a patch of black on the back of his head. He doesn't have a crest on his head like our common blue jays do at home. Apparently, this guy doesn't realize he has crossed the Canadian border that is a few miles away.

It is a mated pair. The female is waiting in another tree. I hold up a piece of bread and she gracefully lands on my hand. I am surprised that her tiny feet are so gentle. I expect her to immediately fly away, but she looks right at me with her round little black eyes and I can clearly feel her thinking, "12 Grain Multigrain—*nice!*"

AJ says the cave isn't much further ahead. AJ is Tom's best friend and they have covered this area a lot. This is my first time in Pittsburg, as it is a four hour trip from home pulling the sleds in a trailer. The trip is totally worth it though; I am loving every minute of it.

Perhaps emboldened by the Genesees, I follow AJ again to the top without mishap. We find the cave, which at first looks like a huge natural depression in the snow. Then I see the tumble of glistening wet rocks that actually form a tunnel down into the ground to the cave below. The guys put on headlamps and scramble down the tunnel. My claustrophobia kicks into high gear. My stomach lurches. I begin to sweat. There is just *no way* I'm going down that hole. Maybe I was buried alive in a past life (just kidding...sort of) but I can't do places that have no clear exit plan.

Tom and AJ in the Tucker Mountain tunnel

I say, "I'm good up here. Don't wait up on my account."

Tom says, "Wow! Look at all the phosphorescence in here."

I call down, "Nope, still not working. But nice try, honey."

Tom calls up, "Hey, there's a bat in here."

I ask, "Does it have white on its nose?"

He answers, "Yes…and white stuff all over its wings too."

I yell, *"Holy $%^t!! Are you kidding me?!?*

I am down the tunnel and into the cave in a heartbeat.

Sure enough, this little brown bat's nose and wings are caked with a white powdery fungus, *Geomyces destructans*. I have been reading about this syndrome for a while now. I know that the "white-nose" fungus has wiped out 90% of our local bat population; it has killed more than a million bats in the Northeast in the past two years. This little guy is still alive, I think anyway, as he is still hanging head-down from the rock face and is not on the ground. He hasn't starved to death yet.

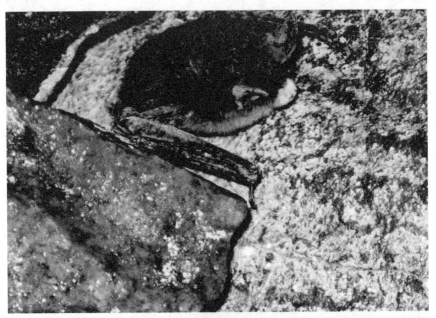

Little brown bat with White-nose Syndrome

"Oh, you sweet cunnin' little thing." I feel like my heart will break.

"Poor little bastard." AJ says.

This problem is a symptom of the larger decline in our ecosystem's health. My theory is that with the milder and more temperate winters now in the Northeast, *the bat caves are not getting cold enough* to kill off the fungus during hibernation (not the other way around as some scientists believe). *Geomyces destructans* grows best at temperatures of about 41-50 degrees F. When they hibernate, bats lower their body temperatures to within a degree or two of the temperature of the cave. If the NH caves' temperatures are hovering around 40 degrees F, then the bats' body temperatures remain high enough to be the perfect petri dish for the WNS fungus to grow.

And of course, the larger impact of losing 90% of our bats in the Northeast means—more insects. Bats eat thousands of pounds of agricultural pests and nuisance species like moths and beetles and mosquitoes every summer. It's terrifying to think about the ways that devastation of the bat population could ripple through our ecosystem.

"I'll call NH Fish and Game to report that the fungus is this far north," I say, feeling really crappy.

On the way back to our camp, I'm consumed with thinking up ways to lower the temperatures in the caves, ridiculous as that may be. Tom is trying his best to distract me and cheer me up. As we are crossing the huge expanse of smooth ice of First Connecticut Lake, he zooms up alongside me and flashes me the V sign.

I know he is grinning inside his helmet. "Wanna drag?"

I nod back, "You're on, Bubbalouie."

On this day, I exceed my own prior personal best. I go a MPH for every year I've been alive on this earth. Medusa and I go like a bat out of hell.

Tommy playing in the snow at Bad Beaver

ICE OUT!

One of my favorite photos is a picture of Tom that I took when the bay in front of our cottage in Surry was frozen over (the old timers said it was the first time that Contention Cove had frozen solid since 1936). Tom was marching around on the ice with the dogs...completely oblivious of the tide that was coming in quickly and making a huge chasm between the ice floe and the shore. (Even the dogs knew enough to jump to safety on land while they still could.) When Tom realized his predicament, he called to me, "Go get the canoe!" I was laughing pretty hard, visualizing him having to swim for it.

What a dubbah.

I ran up to the cottage, only to find the canoe was frozen solid into the ground. However, we did have our long wooden flagpole that we take down every fall when we close up camp. I pushed the flagpole out to Tom, expecting that he would pull himself in to shore. But NOPE... he discovered that he could pole himself around while standing on the ice shelf...like he was the original/primitive paddle boarder. He was grinning ear-to-ear like the Cheshire cat. He went up and down the coast for about an hour, screwing around with the tide and flirting with disaster. I thought he looked like Huck Finn so I took this shot. When he finally came in to shore, his iceberg had melted down to the size of a beer cooler. But, consistent with his calculations, it still supported his weight and brought him home safe and dry.

Tom as Huckleberry Finn

THE WANDERING NURSING PAD

Back when I first opened Longmeadow Farm Birthing Home, my birth center in New Hampshire, a young friend of mine had the first baby to be born there. It was a true honor to be able to attend her, and it was a great birth. I remember a fabulous quote from her during her labor. When she was in transition, she was reclining in the tub with candles lit all around her and soft music playing in the background. A student midwife was gently pouring warm water over her belly.

She said, "I feel like an Egyptian Queen—a regal Egyptian Queen who is writhing around in excruciating pain."

This young woman was a single mom. When her baby was about four months old she decided she wanted to get out of the house and party for New Year's Eve. She got all glammed up. I saw her on her way to the music hall where she was going to let loose for a moment with a well-deserved break from solo motherhood.

She looked beautiful. She had on a strapless black dress that was flirty and a little bit naughty. Her long blond hair was newly washed and fluffed up. She had on eye makeup for the first time in months. Really, she was stunning.

I said, "Knock' em dead, kid."

She said she was really having a great time. She was reveling in the freedom of having her body back to herself. For a brief moment she could forget that she had a dependent human being who was attached to her breasts 24/7.

At the party, she was dancing her ass off. At one point late in the evening, she was dancing with a very cute guy, and they were really hitting it off. She was rocking the moment.

Rocking it until, to her sheer horror, she saw that one of her nursing pads had escaped its confine and was lying on the dance floor at their feet. There it was in all its "contoured shape for exceptional fit" glory. She was mortified. Maybe if she ignored it, it would go away.

She stood stone still as the cute guy noticed the nursing pad and leaned over and picked it up.

He said, "Oh look, someone lost their yarmulke."

MAZEL TOV!

Baby Sam

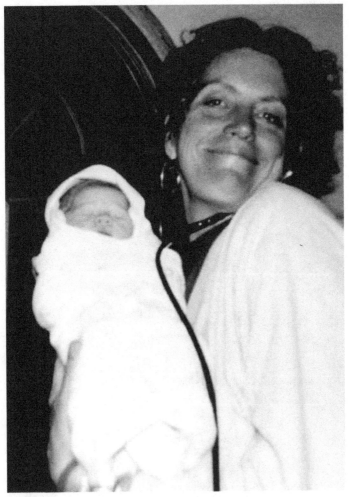

Midwife Carol Leonard with Sam Carpenter, circa 1993

I had been asked to be a guest speaker at the University of New Hampshire's nursing course "Making Babies." This is a wildly popular class, probably due to the number of topics that explore sexuality. This current class was huge, about 250 students, and they were all present on this day before the Christmas break because they were getting double extra credit just for showing up. Most of them were texting during my lecture, which I found to be unspeakably rude; but I guess that's just my Luddite age showing. I pressed on with my spiel about the history of midwifery in NH and in the US, trying my best to ignore the glare of smart phones illuminating the kids' faces.

As I was packing up to leave, a very smiley young man came bounding up to the podium and handed me a white envelope. He was adorable in that scruffy, rumpled "hipster" look (god, I really *am* showing my age). He was grinning from ear to ear. In the envelope was a photo of me—20 years younger—holding a tightly swaddled newborn. I have a very distinct look of triumph on my face. The young man gave me a huge bear hug and said, "That's *me!* My name is Sam Carpenter and you delivered me when I was born. I don't know if you remember my birth or not but I wanted to give you this picture of us."

I looked at him with his impish smile, in his tee shirt and thrift store black suit coat, and said, "Oh, yes, I remember your birth all right." How could I forget? I wondered how much *he* knew.

I had delivered Sam's older brother, Nick, twelve years prior to Sam's birth. His parents were lovely people. His father, Bud, was a farrier and his mother, Jane, was a rodeo queen. She gave birth to Nick in the winter of 1981. Jane was a quiet, strong, no nonsense woman, and Nick's birth was just as straightforward. It was a pleasure to be there with them and I got a year's worth of free shoeing in the bargain. Baby Nick grew into a strong and quiet young man. Apparently, Nick had a gift with horses in his own right, and was becoming locally known for his ability to break and train green horses for riding. He was learning to become a farrier like his dad.

When Nick was twelve years old, he and a group of his friends were swimming in Northwood Lake. Their mothers were standing knee deep in water on the shore chatting and sharing neighborhood gossip, when a drunken motor-boater from Massachusetts came speeding too close to shore. Jane watched in horror as the speedboat plowed into the swimming kids, killing Nick instantly with the propeller.

When I heard of Nick's death, it seemed intolerable to me. My heart was breaking for Jane and Bud. The pain of losing a child was inconceivable to me, a grief too deep to comprehend. I felt as though I had bonded with Nick. As his midwife and the first to greet him at birth, I was forever connected to this child. And now, I could envision only too well the long and impossibly slow road of healing that was ahead for his parents.

What Jane didn't know at the moment she was standing on the shore, witnessing her son's tragic end, was that she was—unexpectedly—one month pregnant. The shock of this realization registered only mildly, as Jane was so engulfed in her grieving and mourning for Nick, she couldn't shift her focus. It was too soon. And as the weeks and months passed, it would continue to be too soon.

As her pregnancy progressed, Jane asked me if I would again be her midwife. She felt that I could relate to what she was experiencing, as my late husband had also died in a violent manner only a few years earlier. I was only too familiar with death and the grieving process. We did a lot of grieving together, and truthfully, going through the pregnancy with Jane was incredibly healing for *me*. We pushed on together through our pain.

The steps and stages of grieving can be painfully slow, and instead of abating, Jane's sadness seemed to increase along with her pregnancy. She was a stoic and wonderful woman, but toward term, Jane's family and friends were concerned that she was not acknowledging the child she was carrying, that her emotions were too deluged with loving thoughts and memories of Nick. I personally thought she was doing a remarkable job of holding up, considering the circumstances, but I did feel it was time for Jane to shift her attention toward the new baby, at least a little bit.

During a prenatal visit a couple of weeks before her due date, I led Jane in a guided visualization to help her bond with her baby. Through guided imagery, Jane tried hard to acknowledge her child within. But although she was very appreciative, she found she still couldn't make the shift. In her lingering grief, she simply could not fully embrace this new life.

Jane went into labor soon after that visit. Driving to her home, I thought, "Either this is going to go really well, or it's going to be really, *really* bad."

Their house was a converted Shaker schoolhouse that they had renovated into a stunningly beautiful home. When I arrived, it was just Jane and Bud and Jane's sister. The three of them were sitting on the bed, quietly waiting. Jane was obviously in very active labor, but she never did fuss much. I sat at the end of the bed and observed the laboring trio. Bud held Jane, and then Jane's sister started singing to her. Her sister's voice was so clear and true, it sounded like a flute. She sang to her sister without stopping for two hours, a haunting, loving melody. She literally sang the baby out.

As Jane's sister sang to her with all her soul, Bud cradled her in his arms and Jane pushed her new baby out into this world. I received the baby and handed him up to his parents. Jane's reaction to her new child was astonishing. At first she stared at him in shock, as though in complete disbelief and surprise at his presence. Then as she acknowledged him and integrated his being, she gathered him to her tightly and began weeping tears of sorrow and also of the greatest joy. Two decades later, Jane would say to me, "I think Sam saved my life."

I was crying as well. It was a holy moment, and I was deeply thankful to be able to witness such a miracle. Jane had worked so hard, through grief and pain, and now baby Sam was here and her life was to begin anew. I sat back and watched their meeting unfold. I think my eyes were transfixed by the candlelight because I swear I could see a soft white glow, like a halo, around the four of them. My tears were from a boundless love of this sacred moment—the entering of a new life.

Now, as my reverie ends, I look at this wonderful, exuberant kid, so friendly and engaging, with his mop of dark hair and the requisite two day old stubble of beard on his smiling face. I say again, "Oh, Sam, I certainly do remember your birth." He grins and tells me that he plans to become an art teacher in high school and a farrier in the summer. Our picture is taken in front of the classroom blackboard. He gives me one last hug before we say goodbye.

Sam says, "I told my roommate as I was leaving for class today that I was going to meet the woman who first touched me."

My heart is melting.

Me and Old Grumpy and the Killer Muncher

I stuffed the last of the old rose-colored wall-to-wall carpeting in the back of Tom's new pickup truck. We had ripped it up in order to make way for the fancy new non-porous "laminate" flooring that is required by the state for birth centers and other "out-patient health care facilities." Tom had already started laying down the new floor, so I was volunteered to drive the tons of ratty old carpet to the dump.

Usually I go to the outside bin to dump my stuff, but the lip was too high for all this heavy carpeting, so I backed Tom's truck into the building where the commercial dump trucks go. I backed right up to the railing that was about 6" high—like the kind of railing found beneath bar stools. I stood at the side of the pickup bed and dragged the carpeting out and down into the trash compactor. This particular compactor was large, about the size of a semi-trailer, and it was actively munching away, happily crushing all the garbage trapped in its jaws.

The concrete floor at the railing was coated in some unidentifiable, despicable slime that was as greasy as Vaseline. I had just pulled the last hunk of carpeting out and given it a good toss, at which point, my foot slid in the grime and I went ass-over-teakettle over the rail. I fell screaming head first down into the Muncher...*except*, the toe of my left cowboy boot got hooked under the rail, wedged between the concrete floor and the steel...*and,* by some Divine Intervention...the frickin' boot stayed on.

At this point, I was dangling by one leg and looking the jaws of the Muncher straight in the eye, so obviously I was screaming my bloody head off. Grumpy, our old and wizened Dump Master, came running out of the observation room where he had seen the whole thing go down. He came running with a long pole that had a brass hook on the end of it. It looked like an elephant tamer's pole. In retrospect, I'm sure this pole was Grumpy's way of snagging trash that he felt was treasure that he could re-sell at the junk sale that was permanently going on in front of his house. Whatever, the elephant-recycling pole saved my life.

Grumpy was a skinny, wiry old thing, but he was *strong.* Scary strong. He fished the pole down to me and I grabbed on to it and somehow he lifted me up. Probably the heaviest piece of recycled trash he'd ever rescued, but he did it.

I was standing there, shaking, barely able to talk. I was blubbering, "My god, Grumpy! I almost got eaten by the Muncher! That f@*%#g thing could've *killed* me!"

Grumpy calmly grabbed some paper towels and wiped gray blobs of grime out of my hair and off my back as I cried. He was muttering comforting words, like, "Jaysus, deah, that was a hell of a scay-ah. What the hell were yah thinkin?"

When I had recovered my composure enough, I got back in the truck and drove home. I fell sobbing into Tom's arms and recounted the story, ending with, "I could've died today in that horrible Muncher!"

He held me at arms length and his eyes narrowed.

He said, "You mean to tell me that you drove my new truck home coated in garbage-slime—and you didn't even put a newspaper on the seat?"

I honestly never know if he deliberately says stuff like this so he gets to sleep alone for the next six months.

My Testimonial for the STAT-Pad (More about Old Grumpy)

I was sent some sample STAT-PADS to use in my birth center to see if I liked them well enough to replace our traditional Chux pads for deliveries. We had a young woman laboring in the birthing pool, so I opened a sample pad and placed it on the bed that I was readying for her.

"What's that?" asked Monica, another midwife who was helping me.

"Oh, that's some new high tech, space age pad that's supposed to have super absorbent qualities," I replied. "It says it can absorb up to 60 pounds of body fluids or something like that."

Monica eyed the pad suspiciously.

"We're not going to put it to that kind of test are we?"

I stopped what I was doing.

"Well, no, actually, sixty pounds of fluid would be quite, um, dead, wouldn't it?"

Monica shuddered. "Want to just use a Chux?"

"No, no. We can branch out," I said. "We can expand our horizons. It's a new millennium."

As it turned out, the young woman labored in that bed for a short while but didn't end up delivering in that room. When I returned to the room early the next morning to clean up, I saw that the pad only had a couple of tiny spots of amniotic fluid on it, so I decided to wash it and re-use it since they cost $11.00 apiece. I threw it in the washer with the sheets.

(What can I say here? It's genetic. I have a long heritage of Old Yankee Thrift coursing through my veins. I can't fight it.)

As I was tidying up the kitchenette, I heard our commercial washer make a terrible noise. The only way I could describe it was a mechanical version of a loud groan. I thought this was odd, but I kept working until it groaned again. This time it sounded *really* bad.

"Oh my god! That thing! That pad!" I deduced cleverly as I ran to the laundry room.

Our washer was a commercial front-loading model with a glass door. I looked in the door and saw what now looked like a white baby elephant inside. A bloated, swollen, doughy baby elephant. I got the door on a cycle where I could open it and tried to pick the thing up. Too heavy. I had to sit on the floor to pull the cussed thing towards me. Sixty pounds, my ass. This seemed closer to 100.

All of a sudden, the baby elephant broke free of the door and exploded on top of me, knocking me over on my back. I was covered by a 100-pound mass of gelatinous, slimy, space-age mystery material. Soaking wet, I managed to slide free and get one of my husband's utility-duty garbage bags. I stuffed the Space Blob in the bag and dragged it by walking backwards out to my Jeep. I was going to ditch it at our town dump.

I waved at Grumpy, our old and wizened Dump Master, as I drove up to the trash compactor. I dragged the bag from my car to the building, but I didn't have the strength to hoist the bag up over the side of the lip. Old Grumpy came over and gave me a hand, and we both heaved it over.

We stood there watching it slide down to the crusher.

"Dead body?" he asked.

"Oh shut up, Grumpy. Jesus." I said as I walked away.

BAD BEAVER PUBLISHING :: WEBSITE CONTACT FORM

(A true communication)

Name: Neville M.

Message: I have just seen your report on stat-pad. This product is disposable product one use product. It saves on multi pieces of paper type products that become saturated. The Stat- Pad will hold any body fluid/washdown fluid within the stat-pad converting it to a gel. The top layer returns to dry within 30 seconds keeping the patient dry and comfortable. It should not be washed **ever.**

Regards, Neville M.

Dearest Neville M,

Oh my, darling…yes I *know* that is the intent of the Stat-Pad…and I certainly *do* think it is a very effective product…maybe a little too effective. My "report" was meant to be humorous… it was never my intent to disparage the Stat-Pad…and I *know* it was meant for one time use—it was dumb of me to try to wash it. The sad part of this story is that it broke my damn washer and I had to buy a new one. But, *my fault* totally for being a ridiculously cheap Yankee midwife.

But thanks for keeping an eye out on your product, that was very thoughtful.

Regards, Carol Leonard

THE RED CANVAS DRUG BAG

Paranoia. It was sheer, unadulterated paranoia that caused me to create the infamous "drug bag" in the first place. Back in the mid-1970s, when I was a brand new lay midwife in New Hampshire, a midwife in Santa Cruz, California, Kate Bowland, was arrested for having Pitocin in her possession. Several years later, at one of the first board meetings of MANA (Midwives Alliance of North America) in Los Angeles, I had the great fortune of sleeping with Kate Bowland at that conference. It was memorable because Kate had just taken her ACNM boards so she had hives.

Because I was practicing in an "a-legal" state, in that NH's laws about attending childbirth were a gray area at best, there was always the perceived threat of being arrested for "practicing medicine without a license." Therefore, I had a little zippered red canvas L.L. Bean bag, on the outside pocket of which I cleverly wrote the word "**MEDS**" in black permanent marker. (Yep, that'll fool 'em.) I put all of my drugs in that little bag: Pitocin, Methergine, Ergotrate, Lidocaine, etc, and all the drug paraphernalia that went with them. I instructed the women who were assisting me at the time that if it looked like we were encountering trouble with the law, they were to throw the secret red bag out the window and feign innocence.

Thankfully, as it turned out, we never had to jettison our drugs. But we dragged that little red bag around to births for years until we finally got certified to practice midwifery legally in NH in 1982. Now we had a formulary of specific obstetric drugs that we could "obtain and administer" according to state statute, so I eventually lost track of that ass-saving little drug bag. After all the political and legal struggles, we midwives were moving on to greater and greater legitimacy.

Fast-forward 38 years later, Spring 2014.

This past winter, a young woman whom I had had the deep honor of attending when *she* was born, asked me if I would be present for the birth of her first child. She, Avalon, said it would mean the world to her if I would attend her. I had retired from active practice but said I would be delighted to hang out with the new "youngsters," the newly licensed NH midwives who owned the Concord Birth Center. I was proud of these young midwives; they were direct descendants from apprentices I had trained back in the day. This gave me tremendous pleasure.

I was called to Avalon's birth in the middle of the night (what else?). Avalon was quite possibly one of the most beautiful pregnant women I have ever seen; broad shouldered, thin hipped, round taut belly with a long dark braid casually snaking down her back; an enormously sensual woman. Now she was laboring fiercely in the birth pool at the birth center. Candles were flickering all along the perimeter of the pool. I became mesmerized as I observed Avalon floating and twisting and adjusting her position to better accommodate her descending child. Such a blessed primal scene.

Now Avalon's sounds became deeper and her groans more insistent. I could see the head beginning to bulge the perineum. The young midwife in attendance rose from her crouched position beside the pool and leaned over the edge to assist the birth of the head. I felt the young midwife tense as she waited. I placed my hand on the small of her back and started gently rubbing her back. I felt her melt into my hand and all signs of tension relaxed and released. Within minutes, a baby girl slid gently and silently into the midwife's—and then the mother's—hands.

Avalon brought her baby to the surface and kissed her daughter behind her ears. She looked up triumphantly and smiled and said, "Her name is Poppy." The room remained intensely silent and sacred. It was hypnotic watching Avalon and her man quietly greeting their babe in the soft candlelight. I was transfixed.

That's when I saw it. There, sitting ever at the ready, was a very familiar sight. On a chair-rail ledge behind the birth pool was **the red canvas drug bag**. *I couldn't believe my eyes!* The word "MEDS" was very faded now. How many hands had held that bag? In what circumstances? What circuitous route did it take to get here in this place and time? How many lives had it saved? It must have been passed down from apprentice to apprentice to apprentice. I started to tear up when I thought of how far we've come from those paranoid early days when we risked jail and our freedom and of the struggles and victories that we have experienced in the past 38 years.

The irony was that now the red canvas drug bag was sitting idly by in a beautiful state-of-the-art, state licensed birthing facility where the midwives were legal, licensed and well-educated—and still giving extraordinary quality care. But now these midwives were supported politically, economically and socially. We "mothers of the revolution" paved the way for them through our joys and sorrows, our failures and our proud successes; we taught them the art and science of our sacred trade. But this new generation, these young midwives, have accomplished even more. They have integrated their profession with modern medicine, ancient wisdom and spiritual practice. Yes, we truly have come "a long, long way, baby."

Of course, at that particular moment, the young midwives had no idea about the history of the "MEDS" bag—so I just sat there quietly weeping and grinning deliriously, talking like a lunatic to a nondescript red canvas bag.

255

SPRING REPRISE

OBITCHUARY

Gladys Louise Lajoie, 1997-2013

Hopkinton, NH– Gladys Louise Lajoie, 15½ (108 in human years), died outside under the lilacs at her residence, in the early evening of May 14. Gladys waited for Tom to get home from work, then she passed peacefully to the great field of fetching rocks in the sky, much to the deep sorrow of all who loved her.

Gladys was born on December 7, 1997 in Hillsboro, NH, one of 10 in a litter of fat, roly-poly, rollicking black and white puppies. Gladys crawled into Carol Leonard's lap to lick some cheeseburger grease off Carol's hand, and then curled up and fell sound asleep. Gladys was named after Carol's notorious great-aunt, Gladys, whom Carol admired as a child for her aunt's amazing ability to perfectly pencil on her thin eyebrow lines.

Gladys Louise Lajoie grew to be an upstanding, conscientious dog. She became a construction worker at the early age of one and was a most valued asset to the crew. She was employed by Tom Lajoie Construction and never missed a day of work for 15 years. She rode shotgun with Tom in the Dragon Wagon every day to the many job sites in central NH. She greeted visitors and workers to the sites and checked their credentials. She made sure all employees were safe and accounted for—and scoped out their snacks at lunch.

Gladys was an avid rock fetcher with an incredible talent for locating the correct rock *underwater*. She retired from the construction business in her last year and spent her time lying outside in the shade, riding in Carol's car and checking out the compost heap for new and interesting stuff. In her last year, Gladys was stone deaf due to not wearing hearing protection on the job. When she barked to clear the back field of possible vermin, her bark was unbelievably monotone.

Gladys's favorite place to be in the whole world was Carol and Tom's farm in Maine. Just two days prior to her death, Gladys made several trips from Camp Kwitchabitchin all the way out to the barn to see what the hell Tom was up to now.

Gladys was a wonderful, funny, brave dog who will always have a bright place in our hearts. There will be an interment service and celebration of her life at Bad Beaver Farm in Ellsworth, Maine.

(This obituary was first published in the Concord Monitor on May 17, 2013)

Gladys's last trip out to the barn to see Tom

HILLBILLY HOT TUB EPIPHANY

Epiphany: sudden realization; a sudden intuitive leap of understanding, especially through an ordinary but striking occurrence.

We buried Gladys at Bad Beaver on a spring day that can be so typical of Maine in May—cold and windy with a nasty freezing drizzle, totally miserable. The weather matched our moods. It was a sweet celebration of her life, though. Several family members attended, as well as a few friends and neighbors who brought dogwood flowers. Tom dug a hole with Maryanne, the excavator, next to Phaedra in the family cemetery. Gladys's body was shrouded in a pristine sheet that was entwined with gay yellow forsythia flowers. Tom carried her into the hole and gently laid her down with her snout facing East. I knew it was hard for him to see through his tears.

Tom saying goodbye to Gladys

We began the ceremony by greeting the four directions with burning sage and a prayer to the four Grandmothers. Several of the group told fond stories and shared their favorite memories of Gladys. I told the story about when Gladys accidentally pushed me off the stairs at the Beave and I landed on my back in front of the sink in the kitchen—with Gladys landing squarely on top of me. (She thought it was terrific that I had volunteered to be her own personal airbag.) Some friends brought very expensive champagne, and we all toasted Gladys, who had lived a long, great life.

In the early evening, after all the friends had drifted away, Tom and I sat together in mutual miserableness. We were going to miss Gladie terribly. Tom sat silently, morosely, staring out over the back field. For some inexcusable reason, I added to the depression by starting to complain bitterly.

"I'm so sick of this effing rain. I'm sick of it being cold and dreary. It seems like it's been raining for weeks now. I'm chilled to the very bone. All I want is to be warm and yummy." I whined on and on ad nauseum.

Tom got up without saying a word and walked around to the side of the cabin. I could hear him rummaging around under the porch. Eventually, he reappeared dragging a large, very heavy porcelain clad, cast iron claw foot bathtub. I'd forgotten about this tub. It was given to us by a New Hampshire friend who was retrofitting his bathroom.

Tom wrestled the behemoth to the fire pit where we had nightly bonfires. He put the tub right in the center of the pit, up on some rocks. Then he connected a garden hose to the frost-free farm hydrant that he had installed next to the front deck. But before he could fill the tub, he had to plug the holes that were left in the tub from the missing faucets and overflow drain. Tom, being Tom, just happened to have two 1-½ inch corks that fit perfectly in the hot and cold water faucet holes. But the overflow hole was a big problem—the hole was 2-½ inches wide.

I have to admit; at this point I was thinking we'd just have to make do with the water level being only halfway full. But I should know better by now. Tom disappeared under the porch again and came back with the top to an old, inexpensive Styrofoam beer cooler. He traced the circle on the cooler top, cut out the Styrofoam circle with a utility knife, plugged the hole and started filling the tub. I have to say right here that once the Styrofoam got swollen a little bit from the water…it didn't even leak a drop!

Then he made a raging fire under the tub with cedar kindling that was left over from making cedar shingles with his shingle mill. Cedar burns like hell. It only took about an hour for the water to get toasty hot. I was a little fearful that the iron in the tub might conduct the heat and get dangerously hot from the fire, and cause second degree burns on my delicate bum…but I was pleasantly surprised that the tub itself stayed cool. The porcelain on the rim was actually cold to the touch. The water had absorbed all the heat!

I slid like a grateful whale into the deep hot depths. Ahhhh. Then Tom handed me a glass of wine.

I said, "Tom, you have no idea how much I love you."

He turned and walked back into the camp to read "Cops & Courts" in the *Ellsworth American*.

Hillbilly Hot Tub

As I floated in my warm and delicious watery cocoon, my reverie deepened. The spring peepers were making a deafening racket with their frenzied mating calls down at the beaver pond. I was astounded to see a light in the sky...a STAR! The overcast skies had cleared and the clouds scudded away to reveal a single bright evening star. It was startling to see heavenly light again after weeks of dismal fog. I breathed in the crisp night air mixed with wood smoke.

I became acutely aware that I was floating in a watery realm above a raging *FIRE*. The seeming impossibility of this spiraled me back to the prayers we had said that afternoon for Gladys—prayers to the four directions. As I floated in my amniotic abyss, I could feel the solidity of my body; my buoyant weight and the lessened pull of gravity. I thought of Gladys's body now in the ground, of her flesh and bones and her skeleton that would become a natural feature and merge with the earth and return to the soil and dust of our land.

I knew at that moment that she had pulled away from us and left us behind. I knew that her spirit was traveling faster than the speed of light back to the center of all Creation. I knew she was going home.

GODSPEED YOU ON YOUR JOURNEY, BELOVED GLADYS

Finding Rhoda

Rhoda at 8 weeks

Gladys had been gone from our lives for one month when I said to Tom that I wanted to get another dog.

His response was, "No. No more dogs. It's just too much heartbreak because we always outlive them."

I looked at my husband and I knew he was still keenly grieving. It had been rough on him. Gladys was Tom's first and only dog, and they had one of those close partnerships where they knew what the other was thinking. When Gladys died, it was the most intense emotional experience in Tom's life to date. Gladys had a peaceful, uneventful passing—but Tom sobbed so hard that he ruptured the vessels in his nose and he started bleeding all over Gladys as she lay still on the ground. The more he sobbed, the more copious amounts of his blood gushed out all over Gladys's fur. I sat on the ground silently witnessing this scene. In the end, Gladys was so covered with Tom's blood, it looked like she'd died a violent, gory death. It was brutal.

But now I was standing my ground. "Listen, my love. I am giving you a two week notice."

Tom leveled me with his "Oh really?" stare with his cornflower blue eyes.

"Really. I don't like being dogless." I argued with myself. "I especially don't like being dogless at Bad Beaver. I want a dog that will be a good watch dog."

Tom sighed. He said, "Do what you have to do. But it's going to be *your* dog."

I first checked out all the local shelters, but most of the adoptable dogs they had were rescues from down South that you could view online. What is it with Southerners and the way they disregard/discard animals? It's disgusting. At first, I was looking for an adult dog; after all, Flo had come to me at five years of age, and she was the dog of my heart. But when I looked in these dogs' eyes, there was just too much pain and fear. I didn't want to inherit someone else's abused baggage. I started looking at puppies online.

I used the Animal Rescue League website. I knew roughly what I was looking for, but unfortunately there were *thousands* of puppies begging to be adopted. It became depressing. I must have looked at several hundred puppies, and I was just about to take a break from it all when I saw a puppy that made me laugh right out loud. I knew in an instant, *this was the one!*

In the description, her name was Reilly and she was nine weeks old, and was a German Shepherd-Rottweiler mix from Clarksville, Tennessee. The blurb went on to say she was born on a farm in a litter of seven puppies that were bred for dog fighting. The four male puppies were taken for the dog fights and the three females were dumped in a high kill shelter. Apparently, they don't fight with females down south...how bloody noble.

This puppy melted my heart because she had a black mask with two golden spots above her eyes. From the photos, I could tell that she could raise and lower the spots independently of each other. This gave her a very intelligent look—when one golden spot was bobbed upward, it looked like she was saying, *"Really, do tell!"*

I made arrangements with the puppy rescue people in Tennessee, those angels of abandoned canines, and I was now solidly committed to the masked puppy, sight unseen. I told Tom we were getting an addition to our family on the Summer Solstice—we were getting a pure bred Shepweiler! Then, I began to stress about having a new puppy in the household. I hadn't had to train a dog in *decades* because when Flo was around, she taught all the new dogs—Gnarly, Stella, Gladys, Phaedra—all the ropes and the rules. Training had been a cinch. But now I was going to have to go back to square one without an alpha bitch to instruct her. Actually, *I* was going to have to be that bitch.

I made the mistake of reading books on puppy training, like "How to House Train Your Dog in Five Days." These were all about giving your puppy a treat as a reward about every ten seconds for good habits. I didn't want a dog who was in love with me for my damn *treats,* so I threw all the books away.

One night, about a week before we were to pick up the masked pup, I turned to Tom in bed and said, "Her name is Rhoda. Rhoda the Rottherd."

He just looked at me for a long time, digesting this, until he said, "You mean 'Rhoda,' as in 'Rhoda Morgenstern?'"

I hadn't thought about this, but I said, "Well, I hope she's just as funny."

The night we went to pick Rhoda up was the night of the "Super Moon," when the moon is closest in its orbit to earth. We left the house at

2:00 in the morning, to be in Plainfield, CT by 5:00 AM. Tom slept the whole way and I drove, directly under the most enormous golden moon I have ever seen in my life. It guided us the entire way. I took this to be a very fortuitous sign.

We got to the assigned Park & Ride just before sunrise. There were a lot of other cars from several New England states waiting for the arrival of the Puppy Bus coming up from Tennessee. Many people stood outside their cars nervously smoking butts. It felt to me like people waiting for a huge drug deal to go down. Then the Puppy Bus pulled into the Park & Ride and all the people eagerly lined up to claim their new friends.

The side door to the van slid open to reveal floor to ceiling crates of crying, vomiting dogs. It's a sad testimony to the plight of a dog's life in the southern states that this happens on a weekly basis. The saintly women who drove all day and all night to deliver these dogs began to call out names and unload the dogs. Suddenly I realized how nervous I was. My stomach was in a knot.

Rhoda's sister, Regan, came bounding out of their crate first. She was large and shiny and energetic and playful. She had been adopted by a couple living in an apartment in Boston. Then Rhoda was handed to me. My dog was small and trembling and matted and mangy. Her fur was dull and lifeless. Her neck was full of bites and scabs. I put Rhoda on her leash but she tried to slide under her sister to hide. Then the Boston couple took her sister away.

I led Rhoda over to the side of the parking lot and she peed for what seemed like five minutes. I thought, "Well, I guess this is a good sign… she's obviously held her pee all the way from Clarksville."

When we got in the car, I said to Tom, "Oh my god, this dog is like one of those pathetic, sick Mexican street dogs." I could feel myself starting to become dismayed. Doubt was creeping in. Then I heard a shout in my head, "Listen. This is YOUR DOG. THERE IS NO MISTAKE AND NO TURNING BACK."

Right. I began to relax. Tom drove, and I sat in the back holding my new pup in my lap and gently stroking and massaging her little body. I offered her some puppy chow that she gulped down like she was starving. I surmised that she was the runt of the litter and hadn't gotten enough food at the overcrowded puppy rescue facility.

As Tom drove quietly toward home, I slowly began to acquaint myself with this new being. I rubbed her ears and laughed at how soft they were and how they clownishly flopped over her head. I looked at the size of her front paws, which were *huge*. Maybe some day she would grow into them. Rhoda trembled and shook the entire time I was doing my inspection. I caressed her fur. I knew her coat would be spit-shine glossy in just a matter of days. I was falling in love.

Somewhere around Worcester, Rhoda finally made eye contact with me. It was as if she had only just then noticed me. She held my eyes for a long time. Then her eyes became soft and full of trust and contentment. She rolled over on her back and gave me her little freckled frog-belly to soothe. She sighed and closed her eyes to sleep.

I swear I saw her smile.

THE DOG AND CAT HOUR

Rhoda and her mentor, the Nocturnal Mouse Slayer

This is a pretty typical night for me lately. It is 2:30 AM and I am awake with post-*POST*-menopausal insomnia. I get up to pee, and on my way to the bathroom, I notice there is a dead baby mole in the dog's bed. A gift from the cat. I look out the bathroom window and see that the chicken light is still on. Damn. The timer must be discombobulated. I put on some long johns and my slippers and a fleece and go out to the coop.

The chickens look sleepy and grumpy. I apologize to them for keeping them up for more than half the night. The new dog has followed me outside, so we take a pee and poop walk while we're at it. It really is lovely out; the stars are extraordinary this night. I wander around outside looking at the glorious heavens while Rhoda does her thing, but mostly she's just sniffing stuff, so we go back inside. She stops by her bowl for a drink of water—at least it's not the toilet again. I take off my clothes and crawl back into bed and close my eyes to sleep.

Fat chance.

The cat brings in a fat semi-dead mouse and drops it at Rhoda's feet. Rhoda begins to fling it up in the air, catches it and stomps on it as the cat purrs benevolently. Rhoda is the cat's new kitten. The cat is teaching Rhoda the subtle nuances of Mouse Torture 101. We don't have any other dogs on the farm at the moment, so Rhoda thinks this is normal. The mouse is screaming hideously. I yell at Rhoda to give me the damn mouse. I chase after her, stark naked, as she runs down the hall with the mouse squeaking in her mouth. She outruns me.

Alrighty then, beastly brats. I slam the bedroom door shut. I crawl back into bed. Tom has been gently snoring through the whole torturous ordeal. It is 3-fricking-o'clock in the morning and I am just closing my eyes when Tom yells loudly in his sleep.

"WHAT?!?," he yells.

"What's the matter?" I ask, startled.

"I thought I heard you call my name. I thought you needed me," he replies.

"You scared me." I say.

"You scared *ME*," he says.

Poor guy. Ever since his epic run with my dying body in his arms, he's been having nightmares that I'm in trouble and he needs to save my life again.

I am just falling asleep when I hear *BLAM. BLAM.* Rhoda is head-butting the door to the bedroom to get in. I get out of bed again and open the door. The cat rushes in and goes back out the bathroom window in search of new victims. Rhoda gets into her bed and starts chomping on the baby mouse.

I give up. I turn on my light and start re-reading a great cookbook about cooking with wild foods, *Black Fly Stew, Wild Maine Recipes* by Kate Gooding. Actually, this was the cookbook that I used when I first started cooking beaver. I adapted her recipe for Beaver Baked Beans, and I couldn't believe how sweet and buttery the beaver was. Why is this meat not considered a gourmet delicacy?

Then I begin to smile. It is 3:30 AM and I have a cat who is teaching the new dog to be a cat, a dog who thinks she IS a cat, a post-traumatic stress disordered husband…and I'm reading about food. It's all good.

Bad Beaver Bean Hole Beans

We do "Bean Hole Beans" at Bad Beaver. Tom made a real bean hole in the ground and lined it with rocks. He makes a raging fire and we cook the beans overnight in the coals.

Bad Beaver Baked Beans

2 pounds dry locally grown Downeast beans
water to cover
2 beaver backstraps
2 yellow onions, roughly sliced
½ C brown sugar
1 T dry mustard
4 T cranberry mustard
½ C molasses
Soak beans all day. Drain in the evening. Parboil.

In Tom's big cast iron Dutch oven mix all the ingredients—except the beaver—with the beans. Add water to cover, about an inch above the beans. Lay the beaver backstraps over the top of the beans.

Put the beans in the bean hole and cover with thick embers for the night. Cover with dirt. The men will mostly sit around drinking beer and watching the fire until they get too sleepy. Get up early in the morning to check (the beans—not the men). Be careful to sweep soot off the top of the Dutch oven before removing the lid so ashes don't fall in the beans (I speak from experience here). Serve for a very hearty breakfast.

Hooray for rednecks and beans 'n beer for breakfast!

THE GREAT CLAM DEBACLE

This all happened in one night this past winter. It did, honest...I am not making this up. I just want to give you a sense of the batshit crazy universe that I live in.

First, a little back-story: My house in New Hampshire has, unexpectedly, been on the market for over two years. We have been driving back and forth to Ellsworth about every other weekend, building our farm, for years—and it is *killing* us. It is ten hours of driving for about twenty-four hours of working our asses off. Tom and I made a New Year's vow that we *must* sell our house this spring no matter what—in order to preserve what little is left of our sanity.

So, with that in mind, when our realtor called and said someone wanted to look at the house again...I was delirious. *FINALLY,* a second showing! Yesterday, I was running around cleaning demonically, which involved hiding the cat box, removing the spinners for target practice out back, shoveling up frozen Rhoda poopsicles in the backyard, disguising the stretched beaver pelts in the garage, covering the bucket of Tom's clams with their necks stretched out about a foot (which is disturbingly uncircumcised-looking for some obscene reason)—all the basics for making our home look like an elegant, sophisticated country estate—and not a haven for a bunch of redneck, borderline prepper-survivalists.

I was just doing the finishing touches of putting out some fresh, long-stemmed white roses in a cut-crystal vase when Tom came home early

275

from a job building a McMansion on the seacoast. While I was very glad to see him, I was also a little edgy (well, that might be putting it mildly). For good reason. For some inexplicable, unfathomable, complete knuckle-headed reason—my dear husband decided that today would be a good day to shuck the 100 CLAMS that he dug last weekend in the freezing, arctic weather.

Too late, I realized this made the entire house smell like unwashed snatch.

We only had about an hour before the potential buyers would be arriving. I frantically threw some Pumpkin Pie spice in the copper kettle that was simmering on the wood stove, hoping beyond hope that this would disguise the clam flat at low tide ambiance. Then I went to my friend Kendall's house to wait it out and drink too much wine.

When we went back home, there was a note from the realtor saying for some unknown reason, the buyees didn't think it was a good "fit." I surmised they must not've been seafood people. Oh well, Tom fried up the clams and we had a great clamfest with his brother, Lee, and his girlfriend.

Then, later that night: I have been feeding our deer. I think that they have been starving during this brutal cold spell. We've never had them come up to the bird feeders to eat before. I got deer grain and apples and have been putting that out every night during the sub-zero temps.

In the middle of the night, Rhoda whined to go out. I, in my sleepiness, went downstairs – nekkid as a jaybird – and let her out. I never thought this (ex) timid rescue dog would chase a deer…but she tore full bore across the field after one. *DAMN!* I ran outside to call her to stop, which she did, but when I went to go back in—I was LOCKED OUT. I had to walk around to the front—naked and barefoot. That guy on TV who runs around barefoot blithely in the snow and ice is totally *bullcrap.*

I thought I was going to have to treat my feet for frostbite. Instead, I crawled in bed and put my feet in Tom's crotch to thaw them out. He was wicked in love with me right then, I'll tell you what.

RHODA GOES ROGUE

Rhoda was a good, obedient, intelligent dog until she turned a year old. Then she turned into a juvenile delinquent. She was permanently expelled from her school when she was 11 months old. I got a call from the principal of the doggie daycare and had to go pick her up because she had started a gang and was teaching some of the other dogs a very dangerous habit. The school said they couldn't "take responsibility" for her any longer. I couldn't believe it. My sweet, docile, former-timid pup had turned into a teenaged street punk.

What I also couldn't believe was, this was *exactly* what my high school principal said about me when I got kicked out at age 16. The proverbial apple doesn't fall too far, as they say.

What Rhoda did that broke all the rules was, she jumped over an 8 foot high fence in their dog yard. EIGHT FEET! They caught her on the outside and brought her back in, and she did it again. Not only that, she taught a couple of other inmates how to make the big jail break…now those K-9 prisoners were trying to escape, too. So the nice people at the daycare said she was too much of a bad influence, the other side of the fence was too dangerous, so they couldn't allow her to remain.

I asked if any other dogs had ever jumped the 8 foot fence before.

"No," they said, and added that they thought she jumped because she was looking for me. I had initially enrolled her in school to get her to become socialized with other dogs. She was great playing with all the dogs, and I personally thought she was the most popular girl in the whole canine class; but now, apparently, she just wanted to hang out with me.

Banned in Boscawen. Rhoda thought this was hilarious. She never went back. Now Rhoda has an eighth grade education.

About a week later, Rhoda and I were returning home from a walk in the back woods. It was late winter and there was still snow on the ground, but the day was sunny and crisp with the exhilarating promise of an early spring. Even though the day was warming up nicely, I was still dressed as though loaded for bear. I had on knee-high rubber Wellies, an old ski parka and my beloved skunk hat. (I made the hat out of a skunk that my mentor, Mutton Chop, and I had nuisance-trapped on the Laconia golf course. I thought it was fabulous.)

Because the weather was so fine, I had released the chickens out of their yard for the first time all winter to take advantage of the freedom of the brilliant thawing day, to relieve them of their boredom from being cooped up for months.

We've always had farm dogs. They've never paid particular attention to the pecking and scratching of our wandering poultry. I wasn't worried about Rhoda as she was mostly afraid of the chickens…or had been up to now. As we approached the birds, I just assumed she'd meekly sit back and observe them, as she had in the past.

All of a sudden, Rhoda broke into a full-tilt, kill-mode run. Like a lightning bolt, she rushed the nearest chicken—which happened to be Sweater, one of my favorite Silverlaced Wyandottes—grabbed her by the head, shook her violently and broke her neck. Then she ran off like a streak across the snow with the dead bird flopping like a rag doll in her mouth.

I, of course, was pursuing her, screaming expletives at the top of my lungs (I will spare you the graphic language). My chase was pretty pathetic, however, as the snow was still deep enough to cause me to post-hole the whole way, slowing me down to a crawl. Rhoda cut through the side woods to the new development down the road and stopped in the front yard of a dauntingly huge McMansion.

There on the perfectly groomed lawn, Rhoda stopped and started to rip the hen's feathers out like a crazy woman. *RIP! RIP! RIP!* Frenzied ripping. By the time I caught up with her, struggling and red-faced from exertion, I thought I was going to die. But instead, I grabbed the dead chicken from her jaws and began beating her with the carcass, swearing bloody murder the whole time. I wanted to impress upon her the badness of her behavior. I also wanted to prevent her from being shot by neighboring farmers if she ever did this on another farm.

I need to insert a disclaimer here: I know the current dog training literature is anti-disciplining your pup. They don't even want you to use the word "NO" lest it might affect your dog's future self-esteem and self-confidence. Let me tell you right here how most of my farmer friends train their farm dogs to ignore chickens. If/when their pup attacks a chicken, they tie the dead chicken around the dog's neck and make the dog WEAR the rotting remains for weeks, shaming the dog. Talk about harsh discipline. I didn't want to humiliate and demean Rhoda that way—so I went for the tried and true method of flailing her with the bloody carcass, screaming bloody murder, caught up in the moment.

Rhoda just gave me a steady, aloof look…with a slightly too bright gleam in her eyes. I knew that look. It was a first kill—blood lust look. I realized that whatever Southern hound mystery DNA she harbored, she was genetically hardwired to be a chicken killer. Pure and simple as that.

I let my anger run out of gas. I looked around at all the carnage in the snow. There were blood and feathers everywhere in the now crime-scene stained snow.

Just then the front door to the McMansion opened. I recognized the owner. He was a financial advisor for Merrill Lynch.

His mouth was dropped open. He pointed at the gory scarlet and various shredded poultry parts in the snow. He said, "You know, Ms. Leonard, this is the most redneck thing I have ever seen in my life."

THE JESUS BEAVER

At dusk early this winter, Tom came in from the barn and said, "Let's go watch the beavers in the third pond. I saw a huge one swimming around their lodge early this morning just before sunrise."

We walked to the upper pond and stood near the lodge on an uprooted pine tree's root system. We waited silently. Tom was standing directly behind me and I could hear him breathing quietly. All of a sudden my heart started fluttering like a schoolgirl. What was this? The fact that he was standing so near—and yet so still? I was amazed that I could still get giddy by this man after nineteen years. *God!* Has it really been that long?

Tom said, "Look. There he is."

The beaver really *was* huge. He must've been seventy pounds. He swam across the pond at an astounding speed. The moon was shining on the water and the light accented the V in the water that the beaver made as he glided silently. The moonlight made it all look surreal and mystical.

I started "talking" to the beaver, making a sound that I thought would pass as beaver language. This really pissed him off. He passed perpendicular to us—back and forth—trying to see who/what we were and whether we were a threat. He clearly was the sentry. I talked to him some more. He didn't like this one bit.

He *SLAPPED!* the water with his tail and dove under.

He surfaced again further out. I talked to him some more.

SLAP!

He was really mad now. I was aggravating the snot out of him. All of a sudden he rose up out of the middle of the pond—like the monster from the deep lagoon—a huge dark hulk glistening in the moonlight, standing on the surface of the water glaring at us. He was walking on water.

"Jesus." Tom whispered.

"Exactly." I said.

Tom said, "There must be a rock out there, just under the surface so we can't see it and he's standing on it."

"I sure hope so." I said.

I forgot to bring my camera and I *really* wanted a shot of this. Tom and I agreed that we would return at dawn to see if we can resurrect the Jesus Beaver, so I could get the photo.

During the night while we slept, the temperature dropped to 16 degrees. We tromped back to the upper pond at daybreak. The hoarfrost on the gravel road was so thick it looked like giant crystals. You could hear us coming, crunching from a mile away. Every self-respecting beaver in Ellsworth could hear our approach like a stealthy herd of over-fed buffaloes.

When we got to the pond, it was entirely frozen over. So much for the walking on water shot. Even if the Jesus Beaver wasn't hibernating in his lodge and he came out and did do his trick again—it would only look like he was standing on ice.

I looked around at the frozen, silent landscape. This was such a bittersweet time of year. It's so transitional. Time seems suspended, winter seems endless, yet there is always the promise of spring. Spring...when this very pond will be vibrating with the deafening hysteria of the mating calls of the spring peepers. Tom and I are in transition too. We're waiting. Waiting to be here with all our heart and soul. This is our land, the place we are meant to be, probably the place where we will be at the end of our lives. We are trying so hard to get to the Promised Land.

Who knows? Maybe we *will* be here full-time by spring.

I sighed. I said, "Sleep tight, brave Jesus Beaver. Be safe. See you in the spring."

Postscript: The Hopkinton house was on the market for FOUR YEARS before it sold and Tom and Carol could build their dream house at Bad Beaver. But build it they did in 2015. You can see photos and an article about the house in Down East magazine at: https://downeast.com/wild-wild-life.

COMING HOME

Carol's paternal great-grandfather, Wellington Parker, who owned Parker's Fish Market in Bangor, Maine ~ circa 1920s.

Am I really from Away? I don't want to sound defensive here, but I feel the need to defend my Maine pedigree. Mainers are incredibly snobby about people who are from "away." Yes, I have lived in New Hampshire since I was six years old, but I was born in Bangor and I come from a long line of bonafide Maineiacs. Maine is 100% in my DNA. My deep love of Maine is too ingrained to have originated with just me. It has passed through my great-grandparents' blood; potato farmers and fishmongers of this rough land on both sides.

Here is my Maine street cred resume: I am told that I was conceived, for lack of a condom, in a little dormered room upstairs in my grandparent's camp, a gray-shingled cottage in Bayside, Maine. (All get-away cottages and cabins are called "camps" in Maine.) Therefore, I believe I have Maine in my blood—I come by it honestly. (Well, pretty much.) Bayside was an oceanside community just below Belfast in Northport, originally founded in the mid-1800s as a "spiritualist" community composed of mediums and psychics. I find it fitting that I was conceived in the former hotbed of healers and charlatans, as I grew up with a hefty dose of the former and maybe just a smidge of the latter.

When I was born, Bayside was famous for its cunnin' old Victorian camps nestled along the Penobscot Bay—rows of colorful, quaint gingerbread cottages that stacked down to the sea. Our camp was at the top of the hill above the common green and the bandstand, with a view of the wharf and the bay.

Stanley and Helen Leonard's camp in Bayside, Maine ~ circa 1950.
This is the cottage where I was conceived and spent my summers.
Looking at it now, it looks like something out of The Hobbit.

My paternal Irish great-grandfather, Wellington Parker, owned Parker's Fish Market in Bangor. I have a great photo of him holding an enormous salmon in his market in the 1920s. He is packing it up to send to the then U.S. President, Calvin Coolidge. It was his tradition to send the first salmon caught in the Penobscot every year to the White House. These glorious spring salmon went to ten presidents until Bill Clinton—who sent it back. My mother swears that Parker's Lobster Pound was the FIRST lobster pound on the coast of Maine. She says it was on the shore just outside of Searsport, and it was very popular. My father, Parker Leonard of Brewer, worked there with his grandfather.

Family lore has it that my paternal grandfather, Stanley (AKA Gunka) walked barefoot out of the woods in Dover-Foxcroft carrying his shoes to his job interview as an accountant with R.B. Dunning Co. in Bangor because he only had one pair of shoes and didn't want them to be scuffed up. He got the job. Gunka was a giant of a man, but quiet and shy, and was completely and miserably hen-pecked by my grandmother.

My paternal grandmother, Helen (AKA Nana) was a large, big-bosomed woman with a white beehive French twist and cat's-eye glasses and false teeth that clicked when she talked. She was loud and overbearing but also sometimes insanely funny. She liked an occasional snoot of Scotch. She also smoked cigarettes but said she "didn't inhale." Her favorite descriptive word was "elegant." Nana bombed around in her little mint green Nash "Ramblah." They lived in Brewer but spent as much time as possible at camp. Bayside old-timers tell this story about my grandmother:

In the forties, the locals used to have Saturday night dances on the wharf at Bayside. They would line their cars up with the headlights on and tune all the radios to the same station and blast the music. One night, Gilley, the local constable, came to break it up because someone had complained about the noise. He was standing on the wharf and Nana said, "Oh, come on Gilley, don't be such a stuffed shirt" as she grabbed him by his belt loops and spun him around to dance. Gilley went flying over the side of the wharf. Good thing it was high tide.

Sometimes I am terrified that I am turning into Nana.

My mother, Louise Homstead Leonard McKinney, was from the Portuguese Gaspar clan in Surry. My Gaspar great-great-great-grandparents are buried in the Surry cemetery. My mom was orphaned at a young age.

Her father rented the Bayside Inn where he cooked and was the manager. Her mother died from cancer, in the front room of the Inn, when my mom was eight years old. Her father died from burns sustained from a commercial restaurant gas range explosion when she was a teenager. Pretty grim way to go—his brother died exactly the same way while working as a cook in Dexter. My mother's brother worked as a cook at the original Pat's Pizza in Orono. (Almost four decades later, after my second husband died, my mother married my father-in-law. This made my mother, my mother-in-law and my father-in-law, my stepfather...but this is another story altogether.)

So, genetically speaking, I'm an Irish-Portuguese mongrel—which is pretty much a set-up for a drunken mess.

My dad went to the University of Maine in Orono and was an incredibly handsome bugger. He played clarinet in a swing band in Bangor. (He was playing in the band the night I was born.)

My mom graduated from Farmington Teacher's College and taught in a one-room schoolhouse in Moscow, Maine. Some of her male students were a head taller than she was.

My mother and father met in Bayside and were married in a little white clapboard church in Northport. I was conceived at camp about two minutes later.

**Carol and her pug dog, Spunky, on the steps of the
Leonard cottage in Bayside, Maine ~ circa early 1950s.**

As a kid in the 1950s and 1960s, I spent the summers in Bayside. I remember the chicken guts from Belfast like it was yesterday. Every afternoon we would have to get out of the water and hang out on the wharf and watch all the white chicken feathers and guts floating down the tidal river from the chicken processing/soup factories in Belfast when they discharged all their disgusting effluent into the ocean. I remember there were always hundreds of tiny jellyfish traveling down the tide snacking on the chicken guts. *BLECH.* What an offal memory.

One time I was hanging out on the beach exploring with my friend, Sally Lovejoy. We found a gigantic beached red jellyfish. I had the brilliant idea to throw a rock into the middle of the hubcap-sized jellyfish. The goo splashed up all over Sally, and it stung the snot out of her. She screamed. I was laughing so hard that I was doubled over and slapping my knees. Sally was so mad she picked up a rock and hucked it at my head. I still have a little scar at my temple that is shaped like an X.

As I have said, my grandfather was a giant of a man but he was extremely self-effacing and quiet. My fondest memory of being at camp in Bayside was of my grandfather. Every time we had a lobstah dinnah – which was often, as my grandparents came from fishmongers – Gunka would tuck two lobster antennae between his upper lip and his teeth, so the antennae would hang down to his chest. He would stick a large lobster claw on his equally large nose and then, making a sound like a demented lobster, he would chase all us screaming kids around and around the dining room table.

My grandmother would be yelling the entire time, "Oh, Stanley, for godsake, stop it! You're getting the kids too wound up for bed. Jaysus, deah."

I'm pretty sure the main reason I was screaming was because it was so completely out of character for Gunka to behave in such a crazy, spontaneous manner. That is what was really scary.

My grandmother had this scientifically proven method to keep the bowels freed-up. She made each of us kids drink a cup of steaming hot clam broth to keep us "regulah" every morning. Then she would wait until it took effect. I truly believe this is why all of us have been in therapy all our adult lives and all suffer from "issues" of chronic intestinal malfunctions.

Anyway, as I have said, my father moved the whole family to New Hampshire to get a better job when I was six years old. I have been away for well over half a century.

I AM FINALLY COMING HOME!

Carol as a teenager at Perry's Nut House in Belfast

Epilogue

I often come up to Camp Kwitchabitchin alone. I come up to write. Tom stays back in New Hampshire building houses to support us while we wait for our house in New Hampshire to sell. The NH house has, unexpectedly, been on the real estate market for three years. I hadn't planned for this. I thought for sure we'd be building our permanent home at Bad Beaver way before now. I could complain and whine and fester about "being in limbo" but I realize that the camp is enough for now. It is still a true gift to be able to be here.

I am sitting on the porch of the camp watching our dogs play-fighting in the field. We have a new dog now. When Gladys had been gone for over a year, Tom finally said he was ready for a new work companion. He made sure I knew that this new dog would never replace Gladys in his heart, but he was ready to make room for a new sidekick. I didn't lose a beat. I looked at probably 500 puppies online until I said, "I found her! I found the one!"

Like Rhoda, she was another very young pup rescued from, yet another high-kill shelter down South, this time from Russellville, Arkansas. Once again we traveled down to Mystic, CT in the middle of the night, to pick her up from the Puppy Bus at a Park & Ride. Her name is Charlotte but Tom calls her Charley—and since she is being raised to be his very own new construction dog, then Charley it is.

I sit here watching Rhoda and Charley thrash each other, over and over for hours. Rhoda has been really great with this new puppy energy. She's very patient. She lets the puppy pull her face off until it gets intolerable, then she puts the puppy's whole head in her mouth and drags her around.

Judging by the size of Charley's front feet, some day she's going to whoop Rhoda's butt. But for now, Charley is madly in love with Rhoda.

It is a beautiful fall day here at the Beeve. The sun is brilliant but there is a definite nip in the air. The cacophony of spring peepers has morphed overnight into the bittersweet sound of fall crickets. I will make the first fire of the season in the wood stove tonight. The seasons move on. As I watch the young dogs, I think of our two old dogs whispering from the Pet Cemetery. I am struck by how life moves relentlessly on too. My life is advancing as well—the cycles are inescapable. But every time I think I am done and slowly going to my grave, something else happens. So I have decided that the gift of aging is beautiful. I am happy here. It is enough now to let the woods teach me, to fill me with the wonders and mysteries of the natural world, to feel my spirit renewed every time I step out of the cabin's doors. I am blessed to just explore in the woods and to let each day unfold as it will. Bad Beaver is our destiny.

Life is good. Life is very, very good.

10 week old Charley slipped on the seaweed at Contention Cove and fell into the ocean and couldn't get out. This is Rhoda desperately trying to drag Charley out of the water by her collar.

ABOUT CAROL LEONARD

Carol Leonard is a midwife, a writer and a licensed beaver trapper. She was the first midwife licensed to practice legally in New Hampshire and has attended close to 1,200 babies born safely in their own homes. She was a co-founder of the Midwives Alliance of North America (MANA) representing all midwives in the US, Canada and Mexico. She was elected as the second president of MANA.

Carol is the author of the best-selling memoir, ***Lady's Hands, Lion's Heart, A Midwife's Saga***, Bad Beaver Publishing, 2010.

Carol is available for book signings and readings. She can be contacted through her Facebook page: Carol Leonard, Author

ABOUT CAROL LEONARD

Acknowledgement

I would like to profusely thank my editor, Jane Hunter Munson. Thank you for reigning me in when things got "too over-the-top." I apologize for random hyphens and using so much "adjectival phrasing" whatever-the-heck-that is. I'll try to quit. Also for curtailing my use of the word "vagina" even though it is an integral part of my vocabulary. You're the best!

The compound at Bad Beaver ~ Winter 2018

~ Finis ~

Made in the USA
Monee, IL
22 March 2024

55516550R00174